The Healing Journey

Through Retirement

THE
HEALING
JOURNEY

THROUGH RETIREMENT

Your Journal of
Transition and Transformation

Phil Rich, EdD, MSW
Dorothy Madway Sampson, MSS, LCSW
Dale S. Fetherling

John Wiley & Sons, Inc.

NEW YORK ✤ CHICHESTER ✤ WEINHEIM ✤ BRISBANE ✤ SINGAPORE ✤ TORONTO

This publication is designed to provide accurate and authoritative information in regard to the subject matter covered. It is sold with the understanding that the publisher is not engaged in rendering professional services. If legal, accounting, medical, psychological or any other expert assistance is required, the services of a competent professional person should be sought.

Library of Congress Cataloging-in-Publication Data
Rich, Phil.
   The healing journey through retirement : your journal of transition and transformation / Phil Rich, Dorothy Madway Sampson, and Dale S. Fetherling.
      p.   cm.
   ISBN 0-471-32693-3 (alk. paper)
     1. Retirement.   2. Retirement—Psychological aspects.   3. Diaries—Authorship—Psychological aspects.   4. Diaries—Therapeutic use.
   I. Sampson, Dorothy Madway.   II. Fetherling, Dale S.   III. Title.
HQ1062.R49   1999
306.3'8—dc21   99-16053
                                                                                CIP

Printed in the United States of America.
10 9 8 7 6 5 4 3 2 1

Contents

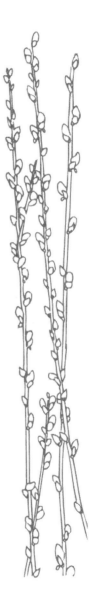

With love and gratitude to Horace N. Sampson, my husband of 52 years, who by his encouragement and example brought this book to a reality.

—DOROTHY

For Gail B. Shaw, forever young and forever friend.

—DALE

To my parents, who deserve and have earned the very best in their retirement.

—PHIL

About *The Healing Journey Through Retirement*

TWICE AS MANY Americans were born in 1955 than in 1935. Millions of people today are entering, passing through, or have completed midlife, and there have never been so many people nearing or already in retirement. The American Association of Retired Persons (AARP) is open to anyone age fifty or older, and has more than thirty million members. Consequently, the issues of *how* to retire successfully have never been more pressing, as the baby boom generation evolves into the retirement boom generation.

Some people consciously plan for their retirement, treating it as the end of their working lives. For others, retirement comes unexpectedly, perhaps due to poor health. Still others are thrust into retirement because they reach a mandatory age and *automatically* "enter" retirement.

Many people who retire later return to the workforce. In some cases, retirement only means leaving one particular job or career and entering a different segment of the workforce. For instance, retirement may simply mean leaving the armed services with a full pension after twenty years of service, or leaving a job because the workforce was being thinned out and a chance to retire early was offered. In these cases, the chances are good that the "retired" are really *only* retired from one career and will continue in the workforce elsewhere. Some who enter retirement *choose* to come back out of retirement. Perhaps they need the additional income, the stimulation and challenge of work, or maybe they feel disconnected and out of touch. In some cases, perhaps they can't handle the change in identity that retirement has introduced.

Still others enter retirement and discover that they like this new life free of the obligations and responsibilities of work. For these folks, retirement is not simply a passage from one job or career into another. Retirement becomes a passage of life— from a life shaped by work to a life shaped by personal choice.

Yet, despite the many books and articles that focus on how to plan for the important financial considerations and worries that might be introduced by retirement, an equally important issue is hardly talked about at all: How will we manage to live when our roles are radically changed? When we retire, we give up not only our jobs and income, but also many of the other important nonfinancial rewards of a career. Being without work changes how we look at ourselves, as well as how we're seen by others in our family, our community, and our society.

The Healing Journey Through Retirement is a resource to help you figure out what work has meant, or means, to you, and how you'll replace those intangible aspects of work that you'll give up when you leave the workforce. It will help you figure out what you want for yourself and how that might mesh with the needs, interests, and wishes of your spouse, partner, or family. This book will help you answer important questions such as, What is it I really want to do with the rest of my life? Once I know what I want to do, how can I make it happen? How can I maximize the many joys of retirement and minimize the inevitable conflicts?

The Healing Journey Through Retirement is neither a guide to re-

Being without work changes how we look at ourselves, as well as how we're seen by others in our family, our community, and our society.

tirement nor a book that idealizes retirement or warns of its pitfalls and risks. Instead, it is a guided personal journal that will help you think about and work through the issues and decisions you face as you near, enter, or experience your own retirement.

The Healing Journey

Through Retirement

I

Embarking on Your Journey

"The journey of a thousand miles begins with one pace."
——LAO-TSU

MOST OF US simply don't know how to retire, and probably we haven't thought very much about it either. Somehow we imagine we'll just toss out the alarm clock, say good-bye to the commute, and then play tennis, go fishing, or just loaf. But tennis, fishing, and loafing, though they can be great for a while, by themselves won't replace your job.

People who've worked all their lives can't easily stop working just because they reach a certain age, and perhaps get a pension. Whether a CEO, a small business owner, a secretary, or a cement mason, if you're nearing or have entered retirement, then in all likelihood what you're saying good-bye to is not just a job, but a career, an identity, and a *distinction*.

Retirement across the Generations

Recent changes in industry, including the job changes and layoffs that have swept across American industry, have changed the face and certainty of the labor market. Changes in the attitudes, expectations, and education of our labor force have continued to introduce evolutionary change into the workplace. Recent trends and studies indicate that people are less and less basing their identity on and deriving their satisfaction from their job. The steady and reliable work so important to the post-Depression-era generation is not only increasingly a thing of the past, but less important to the baby boom and beyond generations who are learning to live different lives than those of their parents and grandparents.

Still, it will take a long time for society to escape the idea that a career is at the center of one's life. The novelist William Faulkner remarked that "one of the saddest things is that the only thing (you) can do for eight hours a day, day after day, is work. You can't eat eight hours a day nor drink for eight hours a day nor make love for eight hours." In our society, work remains a defining feature of our daily lives and implicit in our identity. *Work* isn't simply employment or the physical or mental activities in which you engage while employed. It refers to the *idea* of being employed and engaged in activities that are in some way productive for both yourself and society. Ending your work life, then, is not something that's necessarily easy to do.

Whatever your age, when you're working, your day is outer-directed. *Its shape is determined by the requirements of the job, and its success based on how well you perform in, enjoy, or are rewarded for your work.*

Accordingly, for the foreseeable future, it's clear there is a stark contrast between the familiar world of work with its hierarchy, tasks, and dependable income, and the undefined roles, wide-open goals, and uncertain economics of retirement. Whatever your age, when you're working, your day is *outer-directed*. Its shape is determined by the requirements of the job, and its success based on how well you perform in, enjoy, or are rewarded for your work. But when you retire, your day becomes *inner-directed*. You alone must plan your day and live it, without the boss or the company sending you signals and directions. One key to this *inner*-directed life lies in your ability to define success and find happiness in satisfying personal interests and pursuits, human relationships, and creative mental activities.

Defining Yourself

For all those years, your job was probably how you defined yourself when you awoke each morning, introduced yourself to strangers at parties, and listed information on your credit card applications and income tax forms. When you retire, you lose the distinguishing mark itself, but not necessarily the *need* for it.

In truth, the nonfinancial aspects and benefits of work—comradeship, challenge, purpose, and even power—are among those that need to be nurtured in retirement. In other words, these intangible features of work fulfill life needs that don't vanish simply because you no longer work.

But working, unfortunately, doesn't teach us how *not* to work. Just the contrary. And no amount of golfing will bring back the often overlooked and often intangible rewards of a working life. In short, although we can be weaned from our work, we cannot be easily separated from what our work gives to us. You're still going to need status, satisfaction, structure, relationships, excitement, direction, and all those other parts of the *psychological income* that work provides, which no savings, government check, or private pension can provide or replace. Without work, the central structure of your life may disappear. With thought, desire, and effort, you can redesign and rebuild that structure. It helps to think of retirement as planned unemployment; the most successful retirees are usually those who do the best planning.

Both men and women face the challenges of retirement with handicaps. For starters, there are stereotypes to overcome about aging itself. Some studies show that younger people think that people over age sixty-five are not very open-minded, willing to adapt, or good at getting things done. In many cases, retirees themselves may share these distorted images of their skills, abilities, and attitudes.

It helps to think of retirement as planned unemployment. The most successful retirees are usually those who do the best planning.

For women, there's often an added burden because they may have been disadvantaged in the workforce. Women over age sixty-five, for example, generally have much less money than men. They're also much more likely to be widowed: There are nearly three times as many widows as widowers, but men are seven times more likely to remarry. And, at least in earlier generations, women often had little or no experience in financial planning.

Men face their own hurdles. In our culture, they are often taught from earliest childhood to be guarded, strong, and competitive. Often when men suffer, they do so in silence because admission of suffering is viewed as shameful and unmanly. Men, then, may be less able or likely to complain about retirement woes. Additionally, often having fewer deep friendships than women, men may not have anyone to confide in after retirement, especially if they're single, divorced, or widowed.

Preparing for Retirement

As you're reading this book, chances are good that you're facing, thinking about, are about to enter, or have already entered retirement. You're also probably not quite sure how to deal or come to terms with this new phase of your life. Perhaps you're anxious about how to best use all of this "free" time or are feeling uncertain about the changes that retirement may bring or has already brought. Perhaps the idea of retirement is challenging your very ideas about what you *ought* to be doing and who you are. Maybe you're just interested in learning as much about this period of time and its opportunities as possible and are especially interested in learning more about yourself. This sort of questioning describes the internal work of retirement: how to think about and best make the changes in *yourself* that are often required by retirement and how to make sense of often radical changes in free time, relationships with others (spouse included), and life in general.

Of course, the ideal time to start planning for the *practical* challenges of retirement is during midlife or earlier, when there's ample time to pick and choose among options. But, whatever your age or situation, it's never too late to begin that process. There are also aspects of retirement for which you simply *can't* prepare until you get there. These are the spiritual and emotional aspects that only dawn on you through actual experience. Whatever your experience, *The Healing Journey Through Retirement* can help you define and shape your plans and expectations and help guide you through this journey. And, make no mistake, retirement—and planning for it—*is* a journey.

There are no quick fixes or easy solutions as you enter this period of your life. How to make the best of your retirement is not an issue that's going to be resolved overnight, or even in a short series of conversations. The most productive retirements reflect the amount of time, effort, energy, and thought that you put into the process. In short, the most enjoyable and rewarding retirements emerge from an in-depth dialogue with yourself and with those close to you. *The Healing Journey Through Retirement* will help get you started on that dialogue and on that reflective work.

Writing in a journal gives you a way to collect your thoughts, provides you with a tool to reflect upon and interpret your feelings, and gives you a place to record your thoughts, memories, experiences, and ideas. Regardless of the circumstances of your retirement or the conditions that led up to it, the clear basis for any reflective work is recognition that any major life change has consequences and often a deep impact on every aspect of your life. *The Healing Journey Through Retirement* provides information and ideas and can help you to think about and understand some of the issues and events that surround your retirement and what

Writing in a journal gives you a way to collect your thoughts, provides you with a tool to reflect upon and interpret your feelings, and gives you a place to record your thoughts, memories, experiences, and ideas.

lies ahead. As a personal journal, it also provides direction and a way to think about your life, how you got to this point, and where you want to go from here.

Surrounded by Opportunities

Success in retirement often means finding satisfying and personally productive replacements for work so that life continues to have meaning and reward beyond work.

When you retire, your emotions, lifestyle, marriage, and relationships all undergo enormous change. If you have the right attitude and take the right steps, you'll see yourself surrounded not by problems but by opportunities. If you can hone your sense of adventure, cultivate patient planning, and strengthen communication among your family, you'll not only weather the storm, but very likely make the last third of your life the very best it can be.

One key to a successful retirement is to figure out what your work means or has meant to you. In addition to other changes that retirement brings, the central fact is that you will be giving up your work. Success in retirement often means finding satisfying and personally productive replacements for work so that life continues to have meaning and reward beyond work. A second step involves decisions about how to replace those intangible aspects and qualities of a work life and how your changes will mesh with your spouse or partner's life.

This kind of reflection often involves a process of questions and answers in which you first ask yourself some difficult questions and then proceed to answer them. A journal provides an excellent means for identifying, addressing, and answering questions such as:

- ✦ What are your priorities?
- ✦ If married, how much should your decisions be influenced by your spouse?
- ✦ Do you need to renegotiate your marriage and marital roles?

- How can you cope if you're single, newly divorced or separated, or widowed?

- If you have children, how much say should they have in your life?

- Should you choose a retirement community or continue to live independently?

- Will you stay put or take the opportunity to travel or move to a new community?

Using *The Healing Journey Through Retirement*

In general, it's a good idea to glance through *The Healing Journey Through Retirement* so you're familiar with its format and ideas, but don't rush through it. Although there's no correct pace for dealing with emotional issues and life changes, consider working through one chapter at a time, staying with it until you've completed all the journal entries in that chapter. This will give you time to reread and think about what you've written before moving on to the next aspect of your reflective and planning work.

However, there are several different ways to use the book. If you're working with a retirement or other counselor, she or he may assign a specific chapter or journal entry for you. If you're working on your own, you can choose to either start at the beginning and work your way through each chapter in the order designed, or you can start with the chapters that seem most pertinent to those issues you're facing right now. Each chapter and journal entry in this book can stand on its own, and you can pick the order best suited to your needs. Under any circumstances, complete Chapter 2 ("A Road Map to Retirement") first, as it discusses issues and ideas associated with retirement and will help you assess where you are in the emotional and practical process of retirement as well as pick the best place to start your particular journey.

Making Yourself Comfortable

Regardless of which chapter or entry you start with, you need to decide which conditions and environment will best support your journal writing.

You may not be used to keeping a diary or journal, so you may feel unsure of how to best start. First, regardless of which chapter or entry you start with, you need to decide which conditions and environment will best support your journal writing. Here are a few suggestions that can help make the process more comfortable and productive for you.

- Set aside a regular schedule for working through your journal, preferably at a time of day when you're fresh and have the most energy.

- Take breaks during your writing if you need to. Stretching your legs can also give your mind a break.

- Consider playing some quiet music or other relaxing background sounds.

- Make sure you have pens and other writing tools that are comfortable for you to use as you write.

- Pick a place to read and write that will be physically and emotionally comfortable for you. Do you prefer writing on your bed or at a desk? A private or public location?

- Once you've completed an entry, reread it. Reflecting on what you've written can help you gain new insights.

Using the Entries

The styles for different journal entries in *The Healing Journey Through Retirement* vary, and each entry is provided only once. There may be some entry formats that you especially like using, and there are entries that you'll want to repeat more than once. Feel free to keep a supplemental journal in addition to this book where you can add your spillover thoughts or write additional entries. You may also want to photocopy certain blank entries in order to complete those entries more than once.

Each journal entry is completed by "Things to Think About," a series of questions for you to consider after you've completed your entry. These are not a formal part of the entry but are reflective points that may spark a further journal entry, serve as discussion points if you're sharing your experience with a family member, friend, or counselor, or simply act as a focal point for your thoughts.

The Value of Your Journal

Much of the benefit of *The Healing Journey Through Retirement* comes from gaining skills in reflection and self-expression. As you answer questions or write your thoughts in a journal entry, you're having a conversation with yourself. If you have a problem expressing your thoughts and feelings to others, writing can be cathartic, allowing you to unburden yourself in private. The main thing is that you *are* expressing what you think and feel.

Your journal can be of great value as you work through the issues surrounding your job loss. But its importance is built directly upon your use of it—if you use your journal on a regular basis, it will become an important tool in your journey. As with so many other things in life, the value of an activity depends very much on what you put into it.

Turning Retirement to "Refirement"

Ideally, retirement provides the opportunity to put excitement and fire back into life. It offers the chance for change, new ideas, and renewed energy and enthusiasm. But some retirees, unable to come to terms with being out of work, become dissatisfied or feel unhappy, and sometimes for reasons they don't fully understand. Here, even in upscale retirement communities where retirees have few *money* problems, there are those experiencing many *retirement* problems. Unable to find new ways to fulfill those needs formerly satisfied by their jobs, or learn to make the most of their own strengths and desires, these people haven't been able to transform retirement into "refirement."

In this vein, one goal of retirement is to avoid becoming "emotionally unemployed." As a journal and workbook, *The Healing Journey Through Retirement* is designed to help you find your own way to plan productively, with a special focus on the emotional and practical issues of retirement. Thus, while this book will touch on financial concerns and issues, it is not about investment portfolios. Instead, *The Healing Journey Through Retirement* focuses on your *psychological* portfolio: emotions, relationships, status, and lifestyle in transition. That's because, in truth, no amount of money can guarantee an enjoyable retirement.

One goal of retirement is to avoid becoming "emotionally unemployed."

The Importance of Retirement

The concept of retirement is this: You've worked a full and productive life, filling your responsibilities not only to yourself and your family, but to society. Now you have the opportunity to relax and live your life without the obligation of work. In this regard, retirement is connected with the aspect of aging. This is often part of the problem faced by some retirees.

In our society, despite the fact that people are living and remaining healthy longer, aging is a significant problem. People don't want to age, and older people aren't sure what value they have to the younger society that's now largely controlling things. In our society, people *aren't* revered because of their age or even appreciated because of their status as senior citizens. Even the term *senior* takes on a different meaning when used as a euphemism for old age. But, as this population of aging people grows and expands, it takes on new power and vigor because people *don't* want to be seen as discards, valueless, or as a drain on their younger counterparts. Retirement is a growing issue because so many people now in control of society are reaching or have reached retirement age.

Retirement is not simply a time in your life. It's not just a time to stop working. It's a time of life that marks a *passage* from a life of work and production to a life of personal accomplishment, leisure, and choice. Retirement is the reward at the end of the day. It should be treated that way—especially by you.

2

A Road Map to Retirement

"Work does more than get us our living; it gets us our life."
—HENRY FORD

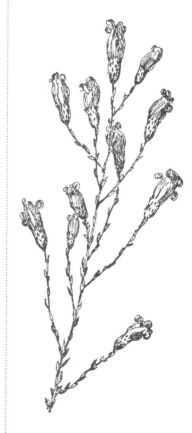

ROGER

As a high-level executive at a resort hotel, I was well paid and well thought of. I had my own table in the dining room and was treated with enormous respect, and even deference, by everyone. I was even placed in celebrity foursomes by the hotel's golf pro and was always well received. But after the hotel was sold and new management came in, I decided to retire. I didn't give the idea much thought or plan ahead. It just seemed like the right thing to do, and the right moment to do it.

Besides my golf and my wife, I have few other interests, and I now feel I have no status at all. Right after retiring, I enjoyed traveling with Sally, but now, although we still travel, I really have little interest in any of the places we go and just want to get back home. The worst part is, I know I can be moody and irritable on those trips, and I'm definitely unhappy while we're traveling, but things aren't really any better when we get back home. In fact, most of the time I watch TV or read, and I've gained a lot of weight. Sally keeps telling me she thinks I'm depressed. I realize how much things have changed since I retired, and I keep wondering what happened to the glorious retirement I thought I was going to have.

BEFORE RETIRING, MANY people see the primary function of work as earning income. But once retired, they miss the other benefits of their jobs: identity and status, comradeship and affiliation, structure and routine, direction and meaning, intellectual stimulation and challenge, and often personal satisfaction. The changes faced by retirees are varied. Perhaps you can live on fewer dollars, but what about the other changes that retirement brings? For some, loss of job and status means a decrease in self-esteem. For others, being out of the spotlight is a curse rather than a blessing. Many aren't prepared for or able to handle the changes in relationships with spouses, family, friends, and former colleagues. For some, retirement begins to feel like the beginning of the end—being put out to pasture rather than being able to live a full and rewarding life unfettered by the restraints of a job. Retirement is the shock you never expected.

Reality Shock

Retirement is a relatively new idea. Almost by definition, most of us have little experience with it. Retirement is usually something that happens to someone else, and for many people retirement is something only seen from a distance—until their own retirement. For many, grandparents and even parents *never* retired, simply working until they became too ill to work or passed away.

With better health care, increasing life span, and earlier retirements (including the early-retirement option now offered by many businesses that are downsizing), retirement is increasingly a possibility and even a likelihood for many. We can look forward, happily or fearfully, to spending almost one-third of our lives in retirement. But a lifetime of work doesn't prepare us for

Retirement is usually something that happens to someone else, and for many people retirement is something only seen from a distance— until their own retirement.

the life we will live *without* work. Although some companies offer limited programs to help their employees prepare for the psychological shock of retirement, most focus on the financial aspects of retirement. Government programs have also placed a great deal of emphasis on retirement pensions and health care plans for the aging baby boom population, but these programs do not focus on the emotional question of what you *do* with the rest of your life once you've stopped working.

A lifetime of work doesn't prepare us for the life we will live without work.

A significant problem with any effort to educate a population that's nearing retirement is that those who most need help—those who have trouble imagining, much less preparing for, retirement—are the least likely to participate. Even financially well-prepared retirees often face great difficulty with the emotional realities of retirement when it finally arrives. Expecting retirement to be just another stage of life, even if prepared financially, can send retirees into conflict, turmoil, and despair as their marriages, family relationships and friendships, emotions, and lifestyles undergo upheaval and enormous change.

A Time for Jubilation?

The Spanish word for retirement is *jubilación*. That's the right attitude, but, sad to say, it's not always what people feel when they do finally quit work. Even if they've put away plenty of money, moving from the demands of a fast-paced job to full-time retirement can be difficult. Why? Because retirees may have spent more time planning for a one-week vacation than for the activities and relationships that will make up the third of their life that follows retirement.

You're possibly feeling anxious or uncertain about your own retirement, or at least curious. That's natural. But many millions of people retire successfully each year, and you *can* be one of them. It takes a little planning and preparation, though, of the emotional and spiritual kind, as well as the economic. Our society is facing a bulge in the numbers of people facing retirement. In the next thirty years, the percentage of people over age sixty-five will nearly double, and the average retirement age is likely to continue to creep downward due to the re-creation of industry and downsizing. More than ever, and certainly more than the generations that have gone ahead of you, you need to consider the fine points of retirement for many reasons.

- *People are retiring earlier*. In 1950, the typical American retired at age sixty-seven. Today, the average retirement age is sixty-three and falling. Corporate restructuring and downsizing are only going to increase this trend.

- *Better health*. In 1900, average life expectancy was forty-nine years. Today, the average is seventy-six and is getting higher and higher with each decade. Combined with a decreasing retirement age, there will be many years in which to enjoy, or regret, retirement.

- *Uncertainty about the future*. An ongoing debate and a constant source of fuel for politicians, the future of social security and government assistance and support for the retiree is uncertain. Depending on a system whose future is unclear is leaving a great deal to circumstance.

- *Personal independence and responsibility*. There's a new national ethos placing more emphasis on individual responsibility, and less on the government or employer, to provide for retirement needs. This may leave you far more exposed if you fail to think about and plan for your retirement.

- *Career versus job*. Many workers in this generation have had far more choices in their chosen careers and have tended to be more in love with their jobs than workers of previous generations. For many, this makes the transition from working to not working even more difficult.

+ *Ongoing family responsibilities*. As Americans live longer and government programs for the elderly are scaled back, retirees are increasingly likely to have more responsibility for their own parents than did the retirees of earlier generations. At the other end of the family spectrum, with the later marriages and later child-rearing years that have often accompanied the baby boomer generation, many retirees continue to face financial responsibility for children still in college, even late in life.

+ *Multiretiree households*. Another marked change in our current population is the working status of both spouses in a household. Two incomes have likely improved family income, but both spouses may face withdrawal issues upon retirement or have entirely different retirement goals.

Two incomes have likely improved family income, but both spouses may face withdrawal issues upon retirement or have entirely different retirement goals.

For many who *do* plan for their retirement, planning has been about money and little else. Although it helps, no amount of money is enough to pay for a successful and enjoyable retirement.

The Five Phases of Retirement

We're all unique, and each person's feelings upon retirement bear their own brand. Some feel depressed, disappointed, sad, disorganized, or angry. Others experience an enormous sense of relief, like kids let out of school for summer vacation.

Although retirement is going to be different for everyone in some way, there are common phases to the process. It helps to understand these because it not only provides you with a language to put your feelings and experiences into words, but also provides a set of landmarks to judge where you are in this journey and what lies ahead. You will also see that you're not alone in any confusion, uncertainty, anxiety, or aimlessness you may be experiencing. While there is no standard response to retirement and no perfect retirement plan, there is a somewhat predictable experience faced by the retiree.

PHASE 1: PRERETIREMENT

Many people have deep anxiety about retirement for many reasons. Sometimes these anxieties are linked to concerns about old age, and other times they're linked to fears about not knowing what to do and how to spend time in a world without work and the structure, identity, and relationships it offers. In other cases, anxiety may be linked to social roles and fears about becoming, or being seen as, useless. Sometimes preretirement anxiety is plainly tied to financial concerns. For most people, retirement is a long way away, a time that will never quite arrive. Then, it starts to dawn on you: Retirement is coming!

As you enter this phase, you face the realization that retirement is not just coming sometime in the future, but is imminent. During this phase, you begin to gear up for your retirement, moving from an initial point of *awareness* to a mind-set in which you more or less have fully *accepted* the idea. During this phase, the primary work involves preparing for retirement and gearing up for separation from work.

Phase 1: Preretirement

For some, preretirement is a time of fond fantasies of a future without the stresses, strains, and demands of work. For many others, it's a time of anxious fantasies, and perhaps even dread, of what life might be like without work. For many, this time may be traumatic, especially for those who have held high-powered jobs where the end of a career is tantamount to death. For most, however, preretirement is a wake-up call and concerns are more likely to focus on income, health, and daily life with little thought about missing the actual job itself. In fact, for most, the idea of life without work is viewed as the fun part.

This is an important time, then. Preretirement offers the opportunity not only to plan financially for upcoming retirement, but to prepare emotionally and spiritually for a major change in the course of your life.

PHASE 2: HONEYMOON

This sometimes euphoric and sometimes rather frantic period often sees the retiree trying to do "all the things I never had time for before." At the very least, this can be poor pacing. Like the marathon runner, you face a long haul ahead. There's not only plenty of time to do all those things, but it's also important to take the time to plan out how best to do all those things, in what order, and even why. It's too easy for early retirees to just throw themselves into all manner of activities and burn themselves out early. This period can also burn out the retiree's spouse, who is usually directly or indirectly affected by the behavior and activities of the retiree.

How can you burn yourself out having a good time? Think about any new relationship and the honeymoon period that predates and initiates the longer-term relationship that follows. Usually, if the partners aren't careful early in the relationship, and aren't especially considerate of one another's needs, there isn't a long-term relationship to worry about or plan for. Also, the relationships, routines, and expectations that get developed during the honeymoon period set the pace and build the foundation for the life that is to follow. People often think and act differently during the honeymoon period and behave in ways they can't sustain later.

Not having a real plan, the retiree in the early phase of retire-

Preretirement offers the opportunity not only to plan financially for upcoming retirement, but to prepare emotionally and spiritually for a major change in the course of your life.

The more unrealistic the preretirement dream, the more likely it is that life after the honeymoon will feel empty and anticlimactic.

ment may not consider the important long-term realities of retired life, such as relationships, goals, and the continued need to experience personal meaning in life. Much like any honeymoon, the period of life without work eventually settles into a retirement routine. The tasks in the honeymoon phase are to show awareness for the life and routine that will follow the initial honeymoon.

As you enter this phase, you tend to *react* to your new retirement, by automatically responding to whatever comes up and acting without any real plan other than to be retired and free of work. However, as you pass through this phase, you begin to react less to your new retirement and move toward a time and mind-set where you're more aware of the present as well as of the years of retirement ahead. The end of the phase is marked by a more *planned* approach to how you spend your days, time, and energy. An important goal during this phase is to both pace yourself and plan for your present and future.

Phase 2: Honeymoon

PHASE 3: DISENCHANTMENT

For some, the honeymoon is followed by a period of disenchantment and sometimes even depression. And the more unrealistic the preretirement dream, the more likely it is that life after the honeymoon will feel empty and anticlimactic.

The failure of the honeymoon period to produce a satisfactory retirement is a failure of planning and choice, however, and not an indictment of the retirement process. The retiree who fails to consider identity, interests, and daily life *after* the honeymoon period is likely to be in emotional trouble.

Equally, becoming totally absorbed in one activity, hobby, or relationship after retirement is likely to place the retiree at emotional risk. Why? Because life has a tendency to throw curveballs. If you substitute making hooked rugs for your old job and then develop arthritis, where are you? If you put all of your time and energy into one friendship and that person moves away or becomes ill, then you're left with no relationships at all. If reading becomes your postretirement passion and preoccupation, what happens if your eyesight begins to fail? This is a simple reflection of the old adage not to put all your eggs in one basket. It's important to diversify, not only in terms of your financial portfolio, but also in terms of your emotional and relationship investments.

There's no specific moment at which one phase ends and the next begins and no set or correct amount of time spent in any given phase. For some, the honeymoon period lasts months and for others days. But this phase dawns as the honeymoon wears off, as it inevitably will. It begins with the realities of adjustment to this new life and an *awareness* that the honeymoon is over and life is now falling into a pattern of new routines. The tasks of this phase include the ability to adjust to this new set of routines and different pace of life and reflect on the emotional and spiritual realities of retirement. For those unable to adjust to and negotiate this new pace of life and set of activities, this stage becomes a significant problem—one in which they feel stuck in a retirement that is unfulfilling, stagnating, and even frightening. For those who best understand this important phase, it provides an opportunity to *reinvent* themselves and begin to redefine their own futures.

It's important to diversify, not only in terms of your financial portfolio, but also in terms of your emotional and relationship investments.

Awareness   Reinvention

⟵———— Adjustment and Reflection ⟶

Phase 3: Disenchantment

PHASE 4: REORIENTATION

Like in any model of personal development, one can get stuck in a particular stage of life. The same is true of retirement. Here, this means *not* being able to tackle and successfully handle the tasks and challenges of any one phase. Those unable to deal with the disenchantment and anticlimax that often follows the honeymoon period face a tedious and unfulfilling retirement. For others, the posthoneymoon phase becomes a time for reflection, an opportunity to take stock of where they are and to develop a set of realistic alternatives. The reorientation phase becomes an extension of that process, a period during which the ideas and experiences of the earlier retirement phases turn into more applied activities and actions.

The reorientation phase sees the active development of ideas and a movement toward a more balanced life and diversified set of interests, activities, relationships, and routines.

The reorientation phase sees the active development of ideas and a movement toward a more balanced life and diversified set of interests, activities, relationships, and routines. The phase opens with your *determination* to decide for yourself how things will be, and not just settle for the way they "have" to be. This phase ends as you move into the next and final phase in your personal development as a retiree and is marked by a sense of *direction*: who you are, how you want to live your life, and the sorts of things you want to do and accomplish.

Determination   Direction

— Balancing and Diversifying ⟶

Phase 4: Reorientation

PHASE 5: STABILITY

This stage *is* retirement. Until now, as an early retiree you've been gearing up and moving toward this final phase, which begins with a sense of what you want to do and how you want to live your life and is marked by a sense of *exploration*—a willingness to experiment with new ideas, relationships, interests, and activities. This final phase doesn't really have an end. In this phase, you're not just thinking about and planning for your retirement, you're *living* it. When you feel comfortable in your retirement, you've reached that final goal of *stability* and have arrived fully and firmly in your retired life. As you proceed through this stage that perhaps has no real end, your tasks are to experience different things and select those that best fit and most satisfy you. Here, the final goals are to truly determine for yourself who you want to be, what you want to do, and how you want to do it. After a pre-retirement lifetime of structure and external expectations, this is no mean task.

When you feel comfortable in your retirement, you've reached that final goal of stability *and have arrived fully and firmly in your retired life.*

Exploration   Stability

————————— Experiencing and Selecting ——————→

Phase 5: Stability

Those who achieve stability know what's expected of them, what's available to them, what they can reasonably do, and what they need to do to remain satisfied and content. Stability occurs only when the retiree has figured out how to deal effectively with change and still lead a satisfying life. Being retired *becomes* a job with serious tasks that require serious thought. It's a job that offers challenge, excitement, meaningful social contact, and personal responsibility. In short, it's a job with both variety and verve.

Mapping Your Position

You may already have a clear sense of your phase in the retirement process and clearly understand what lies ahead, or you may be just tuning in to the possibility or reality of retirement. Whatever the circumstance, the journal entries in this chapter will help you pinpoint your location and the tasks that are the most pertinent at this moment. The first journal entry will help you gauge where you are right now, and the following entries can help you decide the best place to start in your journaling work and this book.

CHECKPOINT: PHASES

Circle the letter that best describes where you are *right now* within each phase.

	I'm not at this point yet.	This is my current point.	I'm past this point.
Phase 1: Preretirement			
Theme/task: Preparation for retirement			
Retirement is just a vague thought.	A	B	C
I'm increasingly aware of the reality of retirement.	A	B	C
I'm accepting the idea that I'm heading for retirement.	A	B	C
Phase 2: Honeymoon			
Theme/task: Pacing and planning			
I'm reacting to retirement without much thought.	A	B	C
I'm recognizing the need to pace myself.	A	B	C
I'm recognizing the need to plan ahead.	A	B	C
Phase 3: Disenchantment			
Theme/task: Adjustment and reflection			
I'm feeling disappointed with retirement.	A	B	C
I'm aware that I need to think carefully about what's ahead.	A	B	C
I'm feeling rejuvenated and able to tackle tasks ahead.	A	B	C

Phase 4: Reorientation	I'm not at this point yet.	This is my current point.	I'm past this point.
Theme/task: Balancing and diversification			
I'm determined to make decisions about my life ahead.	A	B	C
I'm reaching out and developing my life in many directions.	A	B	C
I have a clear sense of where I want to go with my life.	A	B	C
Phase 5: Stability			
Theme/task: Experiencing and selecting			
I'm actively exploring alternatives and new paths.	A	B	C
I'm feeling stable and adjusting well to my retirement.	A	B	C
I'm looking forward to my life in the present and in the future.	A	B	C

Getting Located

You're now aware of the phases through which many retirees pass as they leave the workforce and begin to experience their retirement. But, although these phases describe the general path and progress through retirement, not everyone moves in such a straight line. At times, these phases may flow together, or you may pass from one phase back to an earlier point or even jump ahead. Remember, it's life you're living when you're retired and not some textbook model of the way things should be. Feelings and issues reminiscent of an earlier phase may return at another time, and moods and concerns may shift over months and even years. For these reasons, it's not always possible to tell which phase you are in. Look back at the answers you've circled and use the next entry to help pinpoint where you are at this point along your journey.

Feelings and issues reminiscent of an earlier phase may return at another time, and moods and concerns may shift over months and even years.

WHERE ARE YOU?

1. What tasks are most relevant to you *now* in your retirement or retirement planning?

a. _____

b. _____

c. _____

d. _____

e. _____

2. What do the tasks you identified tell you about your current degree of planning and preparation?

_____

_____

_____

_____

3. Based on your answers to Question 2 and in the previous journal entry, which phase of retirement do you believe you're in?

_____

4. Was it difficult for you to identify your current phase? If so, why?

_____

_____

_____

_____

5. What do you need to most actively address to deal with the tasks of your current phase?

_____

_____

_____

_____

6. What do you need to do to move on to the next phase?

_____

_____

_____

_____

_____

THINGS TO THINK ABOUT

- Does the idea that there are phases to retirement fit your own experience so far? Is it useful to hear that there are phases?
- Are you feeling encouraged by what you've read so far, or does the work required to ensure a successful retirement seem like more than you'd imagined?
- If you have a spouse or children, how are their needs and concerns affecting you and your decision-making process? Have you been sharing with them enough about what's going on for you? Have you been adequately taking their needs and views into account?

Where to Begin the Journey

It may be completely clear to you where to begin your journaling and how best to use this book. It's also quite possible that things just aren't that clear and you don't know where to begin. Although you can work your way through the book in the sequence presented here, each chapter is designed to stand alone, independent of every other chapter, so you can start anywhere you'd like. If you have concerns or issues that are especially pressing for you now, start your work at the relevant chapter.

The next entry will help you to think about those issues, concerns, or questions that seem most relevant now. It presents a checklist that can help you sort out your priorities and select those chapters that most fit current needs.

ASSESSING YOUR AREAS OF GREATEST CONCERN

1. Check off each area that's relevant to what you're generally experiencing at this point in your life. (The numbers in parentheses next to each area indicate the chapters most relevant to that particular area.)

___As a single, widowed, or divorced person, I fear being cut off from friends. (4, 5, 6, 10)

___I don't know what to do without my work. (4, 5, 6, 8, 13)

___I feel depressed and lifeless without a career or job. (3, 4, 5, 6)

___I feel useless without a career or job. (4, 5, 6, 8, 13)

___I find it difficult to let go of my role in the workforce. (4, 5, 8)

___I find myself wondering if I should move after retirement. (11, 13)

___I have no other interests outside of my career. (5, 6, 9, 10)

___I have trouble budgeting my money and expenses. (7)

___I worry about abrupt changes in my life. (3, 4, 5, 13)

___I worry about aging and death. (3, 10, 12)

___I worry about being lonely after I retire. (6, 9, 10, 13)

___I worry about boredom. (6, 8, 10, 11)

___I worry about my health. (5, 6)

___I worry I won't have enough to do at home to keep me busy. (6, 8, 13)

___I worry that retirement will be shaped more by others than my own needs. (9, 11)

___I worry that retirement is the first step to becoming stagnant. (5, 6, 8, 13)

___I'm a fast-paced person, not used to a slower-paced lifestyle. (4, 5, 6, 8, 13)

___I'm afraid I won't be able to make new friends. (5, 6, 10)

___I'm afraid that once I retire, I'll have to give up a comfortable lifestyle. (7, 13)

___I'm concerned about difficulty adjusting to more time at home. (4, 5, 6, 9, 11)

___I'm concerned about how I'll be seen by others once I'm retired. (3, 5)

___ I'm concerned that I won't have enough money to do what I want. (7, 8, 13)

___ Money is very important to me for security and emotional comfort. (7, 8)

___ My life has no meaning that I can articulate. (3, 5, 6, 12)

___ My spouse and I are having difficulty adjusting to more time spent together. (4, 9)

___ My spouse and I disagree on where we should live after retirement. (4, 9, 11, 13)

___ My whole identity seems tied up in my job. (4, 5, 6, 12)

___Without work to hold us together, I'm concerned about losing my friends. (4, 10)

2. Of the issues, questions, or concerns you've checked off, which four seem the most intense or pressing right now?

a. _____

b. _____

c. _____

d. _____

THINGS TO THINK ABOUT

- Do you share your feelings or concerns with anyone else?
- Do your concerns or feelings seem so intense and worrisome that you can't handle them alone? If so, what stops you from getting help and support?
- Do you need any help or support getting through this time in your life? If so, what kind of help? Can you ask for help when it's needed?

Making the Golden Years Golden

Erik Erikson, the eminent psychologist, described the tasks of early and middle adulthood as intimacy, career involvement, and guiding the development of our children, thus shaping the next generation. He portrayed the tasks of later adulthood as reflection and continued self-fulfillment. In Erikson's view, success in later adulthood meant accepting one's own accomplishments and failures, resolving issues, and dealing fully with the reality of one's own life in its entirety. Simply put, Erikson felt that you either succeed in your ability to accept life and live it to the fullest, or you fail to meet the tasks for a healthy and satisfying adulthood and succumb to stagnation and eventual despair.

When you achieve success in retirement, you achieve integrity through the fusion of your life's achievements and failures. Retirees who achieve emotional integration know who they are and what they want. They are confident in their ability to cope, and they can appreciate the possibilities within themselves. Instead of believing life ends when their pension begins, the emotionally successful retiree can enjoy the present and the future with emotional and spiritual questions largely worked out. Retirement becomes a wonderful period in which the windfall of free time is converted to self-fulfillment.

Instead of believing life ends when their pension begins, the emotionally successful retiree can enjoy the present and the future with emotional and spiritual questions largely worked out.

Beginning Your Journey

More than likely, you're experiencing the normal and typical emotions and thoughts that accompany any major life change, and retirement in particular. Armed with that knowledge, it's now time for you to begin your reflective journey, dealing with the emotional, spiritual, and practical aspects of this passage in your life. There are likely to be bumps along the road and obstacles in your way, but if you use this journal, you'll not only have a travel guide, you'll also have a personal and private companion on the road.

The previous journal entry provided a way for you to consider those issues that are most pressing right now. If you want to work on any of these issues or concerns right away, turn to the chapters whose numbers are given in the parentheses to the right of each area. Otherwise, begin with the next chapter and work your way through *The Healing Journey Through Retirement* sequentially. Either way, you may still want to come back to the checklist from time to time to see which issues or concerns are the most pressing at any given time. Whichever path you choose, good luck on your journey!

3

Destination:
UNDERSTANDING
YOUR FEELINGS

"Half of our mistakes in life arise from feeling where we ought to think and thinking where we ought to feel."
——JOHN CHURTON COLLINS

HUNTER

The first year away from my job, I thought I was maybe having a nervous breakdown. I alternately felt angry, hurt, and sad, and I increasingly came to feel empty and useless inside. I had great trouble sleeping and saw my doctor several times for checkups, but kept finding that nothing was physically wrong. I found a great deal of my thoughts and energy were tied up in my old job. It not only hurt me immensely that the consulting firm I'd founded had moved on so well without me, but important company policies I'd implemented were reversed. When I visited, I found my successors to be condescending, as though I was worn-out and without any energy or value. I started to feel that they were changing the firm's direction on purpose, just to tarnish my reputation.

Nothing I did seemed to alleviate or fix my sense of emptiness. I even began to lash out at my wife, and several times accused her of enjoying seeing me hamstrung by my feelings. I thought it probably made her feel more powerful to see me weakened after all the years I'd been such a forceful individual and strong husband.

Eventually, I came to see I had an emotional problem that I just

couldn't let go of, and it was quite literally eating up all my thoughts and energy and clouding my judgment. After that, I started to talk more to my wife about what I was going through, and my doctor recommended a counselor. It took a while, but I was finally able to regain control of my emotions, see things more clearly, and move on with my new life and my retirement.

Feelings don't tell you why you're feeling emotional, but they do give important clues to what's going on inside of you.

FACING RETIREMENT, YOU probably have a storm of feelings swirling in your head, some hopeful, others fearful. Some may be contradictory and confusing. This isn't unusual. In fact, it's the human condition.

Feelings come in every shape and size. Often, feelings are directly attached to a specific situation or event, such as a loss of some kind or an interaction in a relationship; at other times, feelings may seem unattached to anything in particular. Sometimes you feel on top of the world because something good has happened; at other times you just feel good for no particular reason.

Either way, positive or negative, passionate or indifferent, and no matter where the feeling comes from, your feelings are an important guide. They point to your experience at that moment. In fact, feelings are like weather vanes.

Weather vanes don't explain the weather, only the direction and intensity of the wind. Similarly, feelings don't tell you *why* you're feeling emotional, but they do give important clues to what's going on inside of you. If you stay in touch with your feelings before and during retirement, you'll have an important gauge that can help you understand and work with your emotions, rather than letting your emotions control you.

A Storm of Feelings

First, recognize that the idea that the *experience* of having emotions is neither good nor bad. It just is a fact of life. Even the negative feelings serve a purpose. Of course, there are many people who don't want to feel any negative emotions and do their utmost to avoid situations that might lead to a bad feeling, working hard to squelch or get rid of their bad feelings. This can often mean engaging in all sorts of self-destructive or self-defeating behaviors that are intended to numb out the feelings.

In learning to deal with emotions, it's never a goal to find ways to ignore or bypass unpleasant feelings. Instead, a primary goal is to recognize and understand emotions so they work for, and not against, you. Rather than something to be eliminated, feelings (even bad ones) can help you gauge what's right for you and what's wrong. If you're in touch with your feelings and not just trying to get rid of the negative ones, they can help point to the issues that are affecting you and provide direction in how to best deal with these triggers. Unfortunately, some people can't recognize their own feelings, or are only able to recognize their most familiar emotions.

Developing the ability to use your feelings as an aid to personal growth means learning how to recognize emotions, and how to tolerate, manage, and work through your negative feelings, so you control them instead of the other way around.

The Source of Feelings

Feelings come from all over the place. In fact, our own past is often a wellspring for our feelings, and the way we have previously learned to handle and express feelings is a significant factor that determines our emotional responses to *current* situations. In addition to your *past* experiences, the reality of retirement provides a whole new set of influences that will affect your emotions.

The feelings of retirees, or the soon-to-be-retired, may be shaped and affected by many things. Positive feelings may be sparked by anticipation of the future, a sense of relief, and the

Developing the ability to use your feelings as an aid to personal growth means learning how to recognize emotions, and how to tolerate, manage, and work through your negative feelings, so you control them instead of the other way around.

ability to fully determine for one's own self how to spend personal time. On the other hand, some of the anxieties and uncertainties of pending or actual retirement may be stimulated by the enormous changes brought about by retirement itself. Difficult emotions may stem from a sense of:

- being "outside," feeling unneeded and perhaps unwanted
- loneliness and lack of comradeship with former job-related associates
- lost "turf" in which there now seems no clearly defined niche to fit into
- powerlessness, especially if work provided authority of some kind
- aimlessness and loss of goals without the direction and expectations of work
- missing the routines and cycles of work
- yearning and nostalgia, keeping retirees looking backward, instead of forward
- aging, and the fear that aging means being without value or an inevitable deterioration of physical or mental health

The thoughts and feelings that are triggered by these sort of fears or experiences may preoccupy you at times, or even much of the time. You may wish the whole mess of emotions about retirement, and retirement itself, would go away. But your negative feelings probably won't go away without some attempt by you to separate the valid feelings from the bogus ones, the causes from the effects. Getting to the bottom of your feelings doesn't necessarily rid you of them. But doing so may help you to understand and manage them, thus lightening the toll they may be taking on you.

Use the next journal entry to think about the role of work and the role of retirement in your life.

THE MEANING OF RETIREMENT

1. What does work mean to you? Check all that apply, and add other thoughts.

___a creative outlet   ___a way to earn money

___a dreadful task to be tolerated   ___a way to feel good about myself

___a means to keep people occupied   ___a way to get together with others

___a means for self-expression   ___a way to give meaning to my life

___a necessary evil   ___a way to help others

___a satisfying way to use my time   ___a way to produce something important

___a way to contribute to society   ___a way to structure my life

other: _____   _____

_____   _____

2. How much does/did work . . .

a. define the way you *feel* about yourself *(self-esteem)*?

_____

_____

_____

b. influence the way you *see* yourself *(self-image)*?

_____

_____

_____

c. shape your sense of your place in society *(personal identity)*?

_____

_____

_____

3. *Work to me is* . . . _____

_____

_____

4. What does retirement mean to you? Check all that apply, and add other thoughts.

___loss of income   ___something thrust onto me

___loss of meaning   ___time for my family

___loss of value to others   ___time for myself

___reality of growing old   ___time to relax

___recognition of my value to society   ___a way to feel good about myself

___reward for a full career   ___a way to give new meaning to my life

___room to develop new interests   ___worries about the future

other: _____   _____

_____   _____

5. *Retirement means . . .* _____

_____

_____

6. How much does the reality or idea of retirement . . .
a. define the way you *feel* about yourself?

_____

_____

b. influence the way you *see* yourself?

_____

_____

c. shape your sense of your place in society?

_____

_____

7. What have you learned about your attitude toward work?

_____

_____

_____

8. What have you learned about your attitude toward retirement?

_____

_____

_____

Becoming Aware of Your Feelings

Any major transition, such as retirement, can bring on a tidal wave of feelings. Since you first began contemplating retirement, you may have been trying to manage, and perhaps overcome, uncomfortable or unpleasant feelings. Coping with such feelings doesn't mean no longer having them, but it does mean not allowing them to overwhelm you. The ability to recognize and understand your feelings is critical to this goal. Something as simple as stopping and thinking about how you're feeling at a difficult moment can be a useful way to deal with that emotion.

Sometimes it's important to behave spontaneously, without thinking about it. Crying, for instance, is an example of spontaneous behavior that is often a very appropriate way to let off emotional energy. On the other hand, yelling at someone because you're angry, overeating, or drinking too much alcohol are not particularly positive ways to let off steam. These are examples of dealing with emotions in a way that may be destructive to

Coping with such feelings doesn't mean no longer having them, but it does mean not allowing them to overwhelm you.

It is always important to discover positive and healthy ways to express feelings that contribute to solutions and personal satisfaction.

your relationships or yourself. It is always important to discover positive and healthy ways to express feelings that contribute to solutions and personal satisfaction.

The next journal entry provides a checklist of very basic feelings, many of which you'll probably experience during your retirement discussion and planning. You may wish to repeat this exercise often as you learn to focus on your emotions. You might photocopy this exercise so you can use it repeatedly. It's best to complete this exercise shortly before or after a situation that's been emotional for you, or when you find feelings washing over you. Doing so is a simple way to help pick up on and understand a feeling.

MY FEELINGS

How I Feel	Why I Feel This Way
__afraid	_____
__amused	_____
__angry	_____
__anxious	_____
__ashamed	_____
__bitter	_____
__dejected	_____
__detached	_____
__disappointed	_____
__disregarded	_____
__foolish	_____
__guilty	_____
__happy	_____
__helpless	_____

___hopeful   _____

___hopeless   _____

___ignored   _____

___incapable   _____

___irritated   _____

___lonely   _____

___numb   _____

___overwhelmed   _____

___resentful   _____

___sad   _____

___trapped   _____

___vulnerable   _____

___worthless   _____

___yearning   _____

THINGS TO THINK ABOUT

- Were you easily able to pick out feelings? If you've used this journal format more than once, is it getting easier to recognize your feelings?
- Do you understand why you feel the way you do? Is it important to understand how you feel?
- Do you want to be able to regulate your feelings? Does understanding your feelings help you to regulate them?

Thinking about Your Feelings

The entry you've just completed is more a *record* of your feelings than an explanation for them. It records your thoughts on *why* you might have been feeling that way, but stops there. It's very important to be able to recognize feelings if you're going to think about

By thinking about and considering your feelings, you're better able to link your feelings to your behaviors.

them — after all, your feelings usually lead to the way you behave. If you don't think before you act, you may later regret your actions. But, if you're going to learn to understand your feelings, it's important to be able to go beyond just recognizing them.

By thinking about and considering your feelings, you're better able to link your feelings to your behaviors. You stop behaving impulsively or reactively, and you begin to see yourself more clearly and better understand why and how you respond to things, including your retirement. This will put you in a better position to decide what to do next. The following journal entry is another that you should consider repeating. It will help you focus on your feelings and begin to understand them. As this entry focuses on only one feeling at a time, you may want to photocopy the format before you complete it for the first time.

YOUR THOUGHTS ABOUT YOUR FEELINGS

1. List the feelings you checked off in the previous entry. If you picked more than six, pick the six most powerful feelings you identified.

a. _____   d. _____

b. _____   e. _____

c. _____   f. _____

2. Of these feelings, which two were predominant?

a. _____

b. _____

3. For this entry, pick one feeling to focus on: _____
a. Describe how you felt.

_____

_____

_____

b. What situation led to the feeling?

_____

_____

_____

_____

c. Do you understand why you felt that way?

_____

_____

_____

_____

d. How do you usually handle this feeling when it comes up?

_____

_____

_____

_____

4. Are you satisfied with the way you usually handle this feeling? Why or why not?

_____

_____

_____

_____

5. Are there ways you might better handle this feeling in the future?

_____

_____

_____

_____

_____

- Have you learned more about this feeling? Was your feeling more complicated than you initially thought?
- Is journaling like this a useful way to explore other predominant feelings? If you've used this journal format more than once, are you learning more about your feelings?
- Does understanding your feelings help you manage them?

Feelings and Moods

Moods are only thought of as problems when they frequently fluctuate, from high to low, or when the most common mood is a bad mood of some kind.

Some feelings last a while and are more like a *collection* of feelings, rather than a single emotion. Sometimes, one feeling is so persistent and long lasting that it takes over how you see things or deal with situations. These are *moods,* or a single underlying feeling or set of feelings that colors everything for you while in that mood. When people's feelings change quickly or their feelings isolate them from others, they're often described as moody.

Clearly, there are good moods and bad ones—happy, angry, satisfied, depressed. Moods are only thought of as problems when they frequently fluctuate, from high to low, or when the most common mood is a bad mood of some kind. Sometimes, when moods are pervasive over time—you get them often, and they last a while—they begin to interfere with your ability to function and with the quality of your life. At that point, a mood may be developing into a disorder that needs treatment. For instance, if you're often depressed or depressed all the time, and you find that *everything* is affected by your mood—your sleep, your appetite, your energy, your sexual drive, your ability to concentrate— your mood may be a more serious problem. The same is true if you're anxious all the time or angry. Moods can become so deep that they change the way you feel about everything.

As you move and work through your retirement issues, you'll no doubt experience many moods. Most of these you will overcome, but some may seem insurmountable. If that's the case, it will be important to think about how and where to get support, and what and when to share with your friends and relatives.

The most useful time to write about a feeling is when you're *having* it, and the most useful time to think about a mood is when you're *in* it. Accordingly, complete the next journal entry only when you're in the grip of a mood. Look the entry over now, but skip it and return only when you can write about a mood that you're actually experiencing. You may not *want* to write when in an emotionally difficult mood, but this is the challenge and discipline of writing.

Like many of the journal entries in *The Healing Journey Through Retirement,* this entry is worth repeating. Use it each time you find yourself in the same mood, or each time you experience a new mood. This way, you'll learn a great deal about yourself. Thinking and writing about your feelings once is only a start to understanding your feelings and how to cope with them. Of course, not all moods are bad—some moods are lighthearted and fun. These moods are important to write about also, so don't limit your entries to only unpleasant or bad moods.

DESCRIBING YOUR MOODS

1. What kind of mood are you in?

_____

_____

_____

2. Describe your mood in a single word: _____

3. What are the main emotions in this mood?

_____

_____

_____

_____

4. Put this mood into words.

a. *This mood is . . .* _____

b. *If this mood had a color, it would be . . .* _____

c. *If this mood had texture, it would be . . .* _____

d. *If this mood made a sound, it would be . . .* _____

e. *If this mood had a scent, it would be . . .* _____

5. Describe your mood in your own words. *I feel . . .* _____

_____

_____

_____

6. What introduced this mood?

_____

_____

_____

7. How long have you been feeling this way?

_____

_____

_____

8. Is this a common mood for you?

_____

_____

_____

- If this is an unpleasant mood, what can you do to avoid situations that contribute to this mood? If it's a pleasant mood, what sort of situations or relationships stimulate this mood and keep it alive?
- Have the types or frequency of your moods changed over time, especially since beginning or thinking about retirement? In what ways?
- Are your moods so long lasting or intense that they affect your ability to function? If they are, do you feel you need help with them?

Triggering Your Feelings

As you may have already discovered, some situations spark certain kinds of feelings in you. Sometimes those feelings are unpleasant. Other times a certain situation may evoke a warm feeling or memory.

When feelings can be tied to certain kinds of situations, you can do something about them. Knowing, for example, that being around family makes you feel safe and comfortable tells you that this is a good place to be. It tells you that when you're feeling anxious, turning to your family can help. On the other hand, if you know that passing your former office or job site brings back sad and depressing memories, perhaps you can change your route. Knowing your triggers allows you to take more control over your life.

Triggers are those things in your life that activate or arouse feelings and reactions. They can be people, sounds, smells, or situations—anything, in fact, that brings back memories or feelings. Triggers that stimulate good feelings and nostalgia are to be embraced, and those that spur unpleasant memories or feelings should be avoided.

The chances are that many of your feelings are predictable.

Triggers that stimulate good feelings and nostalgia are to be embraced, and those that spur unpleasant memories or feelings should be avoided.

This means you can almost count on them under certain conditions; in turn, this allows you to do something about them. If you know it's going to rain, although you can't stop the rain, you *can* wear a rain coat. The next entry will help you look at those things that trigger *unpleasant* feelings. You can easily adapt it to write about positive triggers also.

TRIGGERS

1. Are there certain types of situations that trigger feelings in you? Name them.

_____

_____

_____

_____

2. Are there certain people who are triggers for you? Identify them.

_____

_____

_____

_____

3. Are there things besides situations and people that are triggers for you—sights, smells, sounds? Music, movies, clothing?

_____

_____

_____

4. What emotions or thoughts do these things trigger?

_____

_____

_____

5. Why do these things trigger such feelings and thoughts?

_____

_____

_____

_____

6. If these are the sort of feelings you want to avoid, what can you do to avoid the triggers? What alternatives are there?

_____

_____

_____

_____

_____

THINGS TO THINK ABOUT

- There are bound to be some triggering situations or people you can't avoid. Are there other ways to minimize their effect on you?
- Are there situations or people that really bring out the best in you? Are there ways to connect more frequently with these?
- Are there other kinds of triggers in your life? What are they?

Self-Expression

The Italian playwright Ugo Betti wrote, "Thought itself needs words. It runs on them like a long wire. And if it loses the habit of words, little by little it becomes shapeless, somber." If it serves no other purpose, your journal is an outlet for *your* thoughts and feelings.

If unexpressed, feelings can, and often do, build inside of people. Sometimes, if held inside, feelings that are difficult to manage

Self-expression provides a means for the appropriate and healthy venting of feelings. Putting your feelings and thoughts into words gives them shape and meaning and allows you to get them out of your head and into the world around you.

can contribute to depression, anxiety, and insecurity. They can eat away at you, and many believe they contribute to physical illness such as migraine headaches, stomach problems, and heart attacks. Emotions can also build up internal pressure until they explode outward in a fit of rage, an act of aggression, or some other external display of emotion. In any case, whether turned inward or outward, few would consider these forms of expression productive or effective. Most often, when handled this way, suppressed emotions become personally destructive rather than serving as a guide to problem solving, self-exploration, and personal growth.

On the other hand, self-expression provides a means for the appropriate and healthy venting of feelings. Putting your feelings and thoughts into words gives them shape and meaning and allows you to get them out of your head and into the world around you. By doing so, you connect to your environment and the people in your life. And, talking about a complicated or difficult situation can help you to see things differently, relieve the pressure of the situation, and feel less emotionally entangled. It's not that self-expression can change the world; it can't. But, it does have the power to change *you,* and the way you see and experience things in the world.

Displacing Your Feelings

During an emotionally difficult day, you may feel annoyed at the first pedestrian who doesn't cross the street quickly enough, or you might find yourself getting easily irritated at something you hear on the news. You may go home and yell at your spouse— even though you may realize it's not really him or her you're mad at. On the other hand, when things are going well, you may find that everything looks great. These are examples of displaced feelings—feelings about one thing that get placed on another.

At this time in your life when you may be experiencing many different moods, it's easy to displace feelings onto someone or something else. Displacement begins when you're not even aware you're having a feeling, or you're trying to squash a feeling and pretend it's not there. But not recognizing the feeling or ignoring it doesn't make it go away. Instead, the feeling gets expressed—often inappropriately—as you let off steam in the wrong way and probably at the wrong person. Dumping your feelings onto others is not fair to them and keeps you from dealing directly with the real source of your feelings.

It's not always easy to put a name on feelings; emotions are often more complex than that. You may find that you're experiencing feelings that have no simple name or are mixed together. Use the next journal entry to think about your feelings, with special focus on *how* you express them.

WATCHING YOUR FEELINGS

1. Give names to six other feelings (or mixes of feelings) that you've had recently that haven't been otherwise named in this chapter:

a. _____   d. _____

b. _____   e. _____

c. _____   f. _____

2. Do you displace your feelings? Onto whom, or what?

_____

_____

_____

3. Do you need to find healthier or more appropriate ways to express your feelings? If so, what might these be?

_____

_____

_____

Thinking Long-Term

Experiencing a range of feelings during times of big change is normal. If you come to grips with those feelings, it's likely that this period will be followed by another that is less emotionally intense. Eventually, your emotions *will* settle down.

So, while it's important to confront your emotions, it's even more important to think long-term. Try not to fret about your state of mind today or this afternoon. This, too, shall pass. Effective planning for retirement requires a long-term focus. Meet your feelings head on and think about them. In that way, you're moving a step closer to self-understanding—and a step closer to clearing your mind for the important tasks that lie ahead.

4

Destination:

THE TRANSITION

FROM WORK

JANE

When my husband retired from his job as a supervising chemist, he was eager to enjoy complete freedom, including endless golf games and his new woodworking hobby. I was all for it and quickly gave up my own job, as I never really liked it. But we soon hit a brick wall. For starters, Harry found that after years of running a lab, working alone at home seemed like solitary confinement. He went from being treated with respect at work to being a solitary hobbyist in a base-ment, and he wasn't even very good at it. His golf also hit a wall after a few months. He stopped finding it the be-all and end-all of his life, and even on the golf course he found himself thinking about his former partners. But, they say you can never go home again. Even when Harry visited them he felt out of place, and on top of that they talked about people and work situations that had hap-pened after Harry's time. He soon gave up those ties.

Unbelievably, I missed my job as well. I didn't miss the work or the demanding customers, but I missed being somewhere and doing something. I missed talking to my friends at work, and catching up on people's lives and just the daily gossip chain at work. I discovered

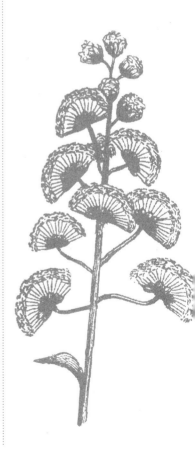

that I didn't have many outside interests apart from Harry. And, frankly, although I love him, I found being with Harry all the time a burden.

Harry surprised me one day when he said he'd never been so unhappy in his life and wondered why he'd worked so hard for so long to end up feeling like this. It didn't take me too long to agree. For the first time in our lives we were free, but it felt like a burden and not a liberation. When Harry said things hadn't gone as we planned, I realized that we hadn't planned at all.

THERE ARE MANY things that will change after you retire. With retirement come changes in your financial status, your sense of structure and pace as you move through each day, and the amount of free time you have. If you have a family, retirement changes your relationship with your partner and your children. As important as any of these things, retirement changes your perception of yourself and your place in the world.

The failure to plan for the nonfinancial *aspects of life after work is at the root of many unhappy retirements.*

Many people enter retirement without really thinking about or planning for their future. Although they might figure out how much money they'll need to live on, people often fail to consider the *other* benefits given to them by their work, such as comradeship, routine, challenge, purpose, status, and even power. The failure to plan for the *nonfinancial* aspects of life after work is at the root of many unhappy retirements.

As you enter retirement, an early step involves adjusting to the changes it brings. Adjustment involves your ability to accommodate this new set of circumstances in your life, many of which involve the nonfinancial aspects, or the *quality* of your life, and your ability to regulate your life around your new situation and schedule. Ideally, it means not just *accepting* and *adapting* to change, but creating a *new* lifestyle that is productive and emotionally rewarding. Under the best of circumstances, this means preparing for the future and thinking about the life you want to lead. For many retirees who don't plan ahead, the reality of re-tirement is an unexpected jolt, triggered by the loss of work and all it offered. Suddenly they realize that their ideas about retire-ment and how they were going to spend their time vanishes.

This period of adjustment and acclimation to retirement is more than just a stopgap measure. It's an early step along your journey of renewal and self-fulfillment. During this early period, your experiences will not only set the stage for your future, but help define what's important, what you want out of your life, and what you want and need from your future activities and sched-ule. A healthy adjustment is an important step in your journey.

Testing the Waters

The ideal, of course, is to think ahead, long before the day you actually retire. This is as true for the activities and relationships that will define the quality of your life as it is for financial plan-ning. Although not everyone has that foresight, it's never too late to experiment a little before committing yourself to major changes or activities that will serve to define your retired life.

Test the waters *before* you give up your job or make a major commitment to change:

- Consider how to best replace the *non*financial rewards of work.

- Think about the sorts of activities or pursuits that might pro-vide a sense of accomplishment and personal satisfaction.

- Try out hobbies or pursuits that you think you might want to invest a lot of your time in *before* building your life around them or assuming they're going to fill your needs.

- Consider friendships and companionship and how these might change once you leave work, and either plan to con-tinue old relationships or develop new ones.

- If married, discuss with your spouse the impact that retirement night have on your relationship.

- Think about how to use your work skills to help others, as a mentor perhaps, or as a volunteer.

- Consider transitioning to part-time work in your job rather than full retirement if your current work give you some joys.

It's never too late to get your retirement back on track, even if you didn't plan ahead. Of course, it will always be easier if you can plan ahead, although that's not always a guarantee either.

What Is Work?

It's never too late to get your retirement back on track, even if you didn't plan ahead.

Look in a thesaurus and among the synonyms for work you'll find chores, drudgery, labor, trouble, business, calling, career, specialty, and task. Throughout one's work life, each of those descriptions probably applied at some time. If the negative ones were more present in your job, retirement offers the hope of relief from such stress and anxiety. If you found your job more a pleasure than a burden, retirement still offers hope, but turning that hope into reality may take more effort on your part.

Income, financial security, stability and consistency, personal expectations, career goals, status and the respect of the community, and self-esteem are a few of the things attached to work. Some of these are *concrete* realities, grounded in the ability to securely support ourselves and our families and live comfortably. Other factors are less tangible. They're more connected to the *idea* that work itself is essential and a fear that retiring might strip us of our worth in the eyes of others and makes us seem idle and useless. In short, work offers many more benefits than just income:

- *Social contacts.* At work you had contact with colleagues, bosses, groups, teams, committees, and departments. In retirement, no one will ask what you're doing or why, and your sense of acceptance and accountability may be replaced by a sense of loss and exclusion.

- *Structure.* Workers operate within an established time frame, determined by the job: when to get up, eat lunch, go home, go on vacation, and even retire. Many employees adopt this rhythm as their own, and it becomes the metronome by which life is lived. That rhythm is silenced upon retirement and can leave a big void.

- *Territory.* Workers have their territory or turf. It may be physical space, such as the office, or psychological space, such as title, authority, or sense of usefulness. Retirees must create a new territory for themselves.

- *Power.* Many jobs contain an element of power, helping to define personal identity. The CEO has power over the department heads, the department heads over their assistants, and the assistants over the rank and file. The only person the retiree has much power over is him- or herself.

- *Status.* Related to power is status: how you're treated and how you view yourself as a result of your position. Many jobs carry automatic status and prestige, such as managerial or professional positions, and jobs can also carry status within the family and community. Being a retiree provides very little status or prestige.

- *Challenge.* Work provides goals and the potential to achieve something. In a job, you become part of a larger group that's striving for something, whether it's making a profit, providing social services, or improving customer service. Jobs provide mental stimulation and, to one degree or another, a use for your talents and skills. Retirees must create their own challenges.

In retirement, no one will ask what you're doing or why, and your sense of acceptance and accountability may be replaced by a sense of loss and exclusion.

Work, then, offers more than just a paycheck. Use the next journal entry to think about some of those intangible rewards you might have to replace as you leave the workforce and enter retirement.

REWARDS WITHOUT MONEY

1. Think about your job. Apart from a paycheck, what other benefits did or does it provide? Once you've checked off every applicable benefit—or added more of your own—go back and rank the benefits you checked. Rank 1 as the most important benefit, 2 as the next most important, and so on.

Benefit	Rank Order
___a marketable skill	_____
___a passion for your company's contribution to society	_____
___a physical work space you can call your own	_____
___a schedule that forms a framework for your life	_____
___a sense of teamwork	_____
___lots of acquaintances	_____
___praise from superiors	_____
___socializing outside of work	_____
___some degree of status within the work hierarchy	_____
___some goals to strive for	_____
___some of your best friends	_____
___the respect of your colleagues	_____
other:_____	_____
_____	_____
_____	_____
_____	_____

2. Take a look at your list. What does it tell you about the other, nonfinancial benefits of your job?

_____

_____

_____

_____

3. Which benefits will you miss the most?

_____

_____

_____

_____

4. Will it be, or is it, difficult to replace these nonfinancial benefits in retirement?

_____

_____

_____

_____

THINGS TO THINK ABOUT

- Were you surprised at the number and kind of nonfinancial benefits your job provides or provided?
- Were you surprised at the way you ranked them?
- What are your feelings and thoughts right now about the loss of these benefits?

Adjusting and Adapting to Retirement

Retirement brings radical change, and this transition will bring— in addition to certain pleasures—a number of stresses and conflicts. Suddenly, you're *totally* in control of your daily routine, perhaps for the first time. You have no one's expectations to meet but

Retirement involves adjusting to the changes it will bring. This is an immediate issue—something that has to happen in order to successfully take care of later long-term goals.

your own and, if married, your spouse's, but this can be a weighty freedom. The lack of external control exerts its own pressure. You're now responsible for structuring your own time, replacing job-related social contacts, finding mental stimulation, establishing status and turf, and avoiding boredom. You will undergo a change in how you're viewed by others and, most likely, in how you view yourself.

Retirement involves *adjusting* to the changes it will bring. This is an immediate issue—something that has to happen in order to successfully take care of later long-term goals. Adjustment involves your ability to accommodate a new set of circumstances and regulate your life around your new situation and schedule. This period of adjustment and acclimation to retirement is an early step along your journey of renewal and self-fulfillment. During this period, your experiences will help you deal with current changes and also help you define what's important, what you want out of your life, and what you want and need from your future. A healthy adjustment is an important step in your journey.

Adapting is a key element in adjustment and may mean making the necessary changes in yourself to work with and survive change in your environment, learning to work *with* change, rather than against it. Where adjustment is about settling into change, adaptation is about personal flexibility. People unable to change themselves to fit new circumstances may not prove resilient enough to meet the challenges of a world that has changed around them. Use the next journal entry to think about your adjustment and your ability to adapt to your actual or pending retirement.

ADJUSTING AND ADAPTING

1. Describe five things that are difficult to adjust to.

a. _____

b. _____

c. _____

d. _____

e. _____

2. What are the most difficult things to adapt to?

___being alone more of the time   ___having less money

___boredom   ___having nothing to do

___changes in relationship with spouse   ___having to do things I don't want to do

___feeling disempowered   ___lack of structure

___feeling useless   ___not having a clearly defined identity

___free time   ___not having a job to go to every day

___getting used to being home all day   ___sense of being disconnected

other _____   _____

_____   _____

_____   _____

_____   _____

THINGS TO THINK ABOUT

- Is this a good time to take on or test out projects, tasks, or interests that you've been trying to find time for?
- In your adjustment to retirement, how important is your family as a source of support and encouragement?
- Do you feel stuck, unable to deal with this new situation? Do you need some help figuring out how to get unstuck?

Problems Versus Opportunity

Whether planned or thrust upon you, change is inevitable. In dealing with change, the goal is *not* to eliminate change, but to learn to identify and manage it. Yet, for some people, change becomes a crisis. Here, it's interesting to note that the Chinese written word for *crisis* is composed of two symbols. Together, these icons provide insight into the two possible faces of the crisis of change: one icon translates into danger, and the other means opportunity.

As well as providing more time, greater freedom, and mobility, retirement also demands that you be responsible for managing your own life and fill the holes left by work.

A primary task in retirement is learning to wean yourself away from work and all it offered you. By now, you have a sense of what all those things were—not so you can pine over the loss, but rather so you can find important and satisfying new benefits in your life. For some, retirement is a constant battle against feeling empty and without value, structure, or meaning. For others, it's a time of *jubilación*. Like every situation, retirement poses problems, but it also presents opportunities. As well as providing more time, greater freedom, and mobility, retirement also demands that you be responsible for managing your own life and fill the holes left by work. You need to ask yourself: Now that I can do as I please, what am I pleased to do?

Too many people don't ask or can't answer that question. Too many fail to seize opportunity. Have you considered the problems and opportunities offered by retirement? Use the next entry to think about problems, opportunities, and, perhaps most of all, your attitude about the problems and opportunities of retirement.

CLOUDS AND SILVER LININGS

1. What are the problems you might face, or are facing, in your retirement?

_____

_____

_____

2. Are these problems that can be overcome? How?

_____

_____

_____

3. What will your retirement be like if you're unable to deal with or overcome these problems?

_____

_____

_____

_____

4. What are you most looking forward to in retirement?

_____

_____

_____

_____

5. Name five of the opportunities of retirement.

a. _____

b. _____

c. _____

d. _____

e. _____

6. What's more likely to motivate and affect you: the problems of retirement or the opportunities?

_____

_____

_____

_____

_____

7. What will your retirement be like if you allow the problem areas to get in the way of the opportunities?

_____

_____

_____

_____

_____

THINGS TO THINK ABOUT

- Has this entry helped you to consider how to overcome difficulties and work toward a successful retirement? How hard are you will willing to work to make your retirement a success?
- What has this journal entry helped you to discover about your attitude toward the problems and opportunities of retirement?

Retirement Cometh

People who develop interests outside of work *before* they retire are likely to make the best transition from work to retirement. On the other hand, those who have little time for anything else outside of their job are likely to feel the greatest loss when the office door shuts behind them.

If you haven't yet retired, use the next entry to think about your retirement and how to best plan for the time and freedom you'll have on your hands. If you've *already* retired, use the entry to consider what *might* be different if you had to plan for your retirement all over again.

WHEN THE DAY COMES

1. *When I think of retirement, I think of . . .* _____

_____

_____

2. *With each day that retirement draws closer, I get more . . .* _____

_____

_____

3. *I very much want my retirement to be . . .* _____

_____

_____

4. *What I'm doing now to make my retirement great is . . .* _____

_____

_____

5. *Other actions I could be taking to further my dream include . . .* _____

_____

_____

6. *Obstacles to my taking these actions include . . .* _____

_____

_____

7. *Looking back five years from now, I think I'll view my retirement years as . . .* _____

_____

_____

8. *The three things I expect to miss the most about work are* . . . _____

   a. _____

   b. _____

   c. _____

9. *I can lessen the effects of those losses by* . . . _____

_____

_____

_____

_____

THINGS TO THINK ABOUT

- Does it help to look ahead into your future? Can you see what you need to do now to take responsibility for your own retirement and make it great?
- If already retired, can you see now what you *could* have done to plan ahead? More to the point, can you see what you *can* do now to make your retirement great?
- One way or the other, are you taking enough responsibility for your retirement?

Visualizing Success

If you've retired already, use the following journal entry to recollect that last day at work and the days that followed. Think about how it felt *then,* and how it feels *now.* As you complete the entry, think about how you can build an even better retirement than the one you already have or turn around and revitalize a retirement that isn't really working well for you.

If your retirement is still ahead, use your imagination to think about the sort of retirement you'd like to have and visualize the sort of problems you might face and those things you can do *now* to bring that future into reality when the time comes. Forewarned is forearmed.

WHEN THE DAY CAME

1. *As my retirement date neared, I felt . . .* _____

_____

_____

2. *On my last day at work, my reaction was . . .* _____

_____

_____

3. *On my first day as a retiree, I . . .* _____

_____

_____

4. *Since then, I have become . . .* _____

_____

_____

5. *What I miss most about work is . . .* _____

_____

_____

6. *Since retirement, my life has changed most because of . . .* _____

_____

_____

7. *I have had the most trouble adjusting to . . .* _____

_____

_____

8. *Three things that are interfering with my ability to adjust are:*

a. _____

b. _____

c. _____

9. *Some things I can do to help me get over these hurdles are . . .* _____

_____

_____

_____

Replacing the Benefits

To develop new friends, you might decide to join social organizations or associations that can help you to make new social contacts and build new friendships.

You used the first journal entry in this chapter, "Rewards without Money," to think about those nonfinancial rewards of your work, and then you ranked them, starting with the most important benefit.

Now that you've entered or are entering retirement, those benefits of work will disappear from your life unless you find a way to keep them alive in your *new* life as a retiree. This is one of those challenges to be faced if you're going to ensure that your retirement is as rewarding as your working life, or perhaps *more* rewarding. Look back now at the list you created in your earlier entry and think about how to maintain each benefit in your retirement or replace it with a benefit that's equally or more satisfying.

For example, if one of the items you checked as a top benefit was "lots of acquaintances" or "some of your best friends," think of ways to maintain these relationships or to develop new friendships. For instance, to keep old friendships alive, you might consider hosting a dinner party, having a reunion with old friends, or just getting together on a regular basis. To develop new friends, you might decide to join social organizations or associations that can help you to make new social contacts and build new friendships. Use this journal entry to think about your four top-ranked benefits and how to keep each one alive, fresh, and fulfilling.

STAYING ALIVE

1. What work-related benefit did you rank as most important or most satisfying?

_____

Name three things you can do to keep this benefit alive in your retired life.

_____

_____

_____

2. What work-related benefit did you rank as second most important or most satisfying?

_____

Name three things you can do to keep this benefit alive in your retired life.

_____

_____

_____

3. Name the third-ranked benefit:

_____

Name three things you can do to keep this benefit alive.

_____

_____

_____

4. Now name the fourth-ranked benefit:

_____

Name three things you can do to keep this benefit alive.

_____

_____

_____

5. What obstacles can you imagine standing in the way of keeping these nonfinancial rewards alive, or introducing them, in your retired life?

_____

_____

_____

_____

_____

6. Is it important to keep these "quality of life" benefits in your life? What will life be like without them?

_____

_____

_____

_____

_____

THINGS TO THINK ABOUT

- Do you have a sense of what you might miss about work? Do you have ideas about how to keep alive some of the things that you *most* liked about work?
- Do you think you have a good action plan to keep your retirement alive and fresh? Do you need to refine it further?

Your Changing Self

Your journal is a perfect tool for noting and reflecting upon change.
Use the final journal entry in this chapter to capture and describe
your feelings and thoughts about this important time in your life.

CHECKPOINT: YOUR CHANGING SELF

1. If you were to take a photograph of your life at this time, what image would most capture the changes?

_____

_____

_____

2. What favorite quotation, verse, or poem best summarizes your feelings and experiences with change at this time?

_____

_____

_____

3. Is there a favorite piece of music that captures the flavor and emotion of this time in your life?

_____

_____

_____

4. Think about the images, words, and music you chose. What do your choices tell you about your reactions to this time in your life?

_____

_____

_____

5. *As I complete this chapter, I feel like . . .* _____

_____

6. *Right now, I'd like to . . .* _____

_____

7. *My most important current task is . . .* _____

_____

8. *I feel like I most need to work on . . .* _____

_____

THINGS TO THINK ABOUT

- Are there specific questions you need to answer for yourself before continuing with *The Healing Journey Through Retirement*?
- Do you have a clear sense of the sort of issues, feelings, and tasks that you'll be facing as you enter and work through this passage in your life?

5

Destination:

ACCEPTING A NEW ROLE

ANGELA

After I retired from many years as a nurse, I found myself with a large, and largely empty, home. So, after some thought, I decided to open my home as a shelter for battered women and rape victims. I knew the women needed the help, and I also knew I would enjoy the sense of service and the companionship. At first, the county was thrilled, and they praised my credentials and altruism—until they learned I was seventy-six. Then they turned a deaf ear, as though I couldn't do the job or handle the responsibilities. But from my many years of practical experience, I knew that where there's a will there's always a way. I teamed up with one of my younger sisters and eventually got my home certified as a county approved refuge.

JAY

I got fed up with my kids, even my own grandchildren, constantly reminding me that I'm not a kid anymore, as though I didn't already know that. I was seventy-one, and they were afraid that I wasn't taking good enough care of my health. More than that, they didn't think I could take care of myself. Tell you the truth, I was more afraid I wasn't taking good enough care of my life, especially since my wife had died three years before and left me feeling alone. Never stopped me though, and in the deepest winter I went bobsledding down the steepest hill in town. I became an avid year-round hiker, and I learned to sail a boat in the bay. And, despite my family's dire predictions, I lived to tell the tale, and even grew emotionally. I got another version of that same tired message from the kids again when I decided to take banjo lessons, something else I'd wanted to do my entire life: "At your age? Don't be ridiculous." Ridiculous or not, I did it and enjoyed every tinny tune I could manage to strum. I was learning to play my own song, not just with my banjo, but with my life.

Acceptance means acknowledging change and learning how to tolerate and embrace it.

RETIREMENT IS A time for change, and many things are changing. For one thing, you're getting older, and for another, as you leave work you change roles. Regardless of how you may feel about your retirement itself, as most people would probably prefer *not* to age, this particular aspect of change is likely one you'd rather avoid. But you can't avoid it, and recognizing the differences between what you *can* and *can't* change is an important ingredient in acceptance and personal growth. This passage actually marks the evolution of your life, and the beginning of some exciting opportunities for personal growth and development. Retirement is more than a change from work to nonwork. It's also a journey of the mind.

First and foremost, acceptance means acknowledging change and learning how to tolerate and embrace it. This is often not so easy, and people develop all sorts of ways to avoid change, or at least ways to avoid dealing with it. Acceptance doesn't mean giving in. It doesn't mean liking or enjoying all of the new realities that may accompany a change. It certainly doesn't mean becoming subservient to those new realities. But to move *beyond* simple acceptance, you have to be able to define change so that it *serves,* and not represses, you.

What is it that *you* have to accept as you enter your retirement? Use the first journal entry in this chapter to think about acceptance. This is an entry you can use repeatedly to explore your experiences at this time in your life, so you might want to photocopy the blank before completing it for the first time.

ACCEPTANCE

"Grant me the serenity to accept the things I cannot change, courage to change the things I can, and wisdom to know the difference."
—REINHOLD NIEBUHR

1. Name four things that are difficult to accept during this time in your life.

a. _____

b. _____

c. _____

d. _____

2. Pick one of these items to focus on for the remainder of this entry. Name the item, and describe why you picked it.

_____

_____

_____

_____

3. What is the most difficult thing to accept about this time in your life?

_____

_____

_____

_____

4. What does this thing represent for you?

_____

_____

_____

_____

5. What is it like to have to accept this reality in your life?

_____

_____

_____

_____

6. Is there a way to reframe this part of your life so it's easier to accept?

_____

_____

_____

_____

7. Review the verse that opens this entry. Is this a thing you *can* change, or a thing you *can't* change?

_____

_____

_____

THINGS TO THINK ABOUT

- It's not always easy to distinguish between things we can change and things we can't. Can you tell the difference in this case?
- Do you usually have trouble accepting change or things outside of your control? Is it especially difficult to accept current changes and events?
- How can you best learn to deal with and accept change? What will happen if you can't or don't want to fully accept current changes?

Changing Roles

In our society, both work and age play huge parts in the roles we take on and the roles that are assigned to us. These twin factors of work and age become large parts of our identities. We almost automatically ask new acquaintances what they do for a living, and it's standard fare to ask children what they want to be when they grow up. Elementary and middle school students are encouraged to think about their career choices, and it's almost a must for high school students. When we ask long lost friends what they're doing nowadays, we are, in part, asking about their work. As John Lennon once said, "Work is life, you know."

The other aspect in this duo of change is age. We live in a culture almost obsessed with youth, in which the aging process itself is feared and senior citizens often feel disregarded and shunned. Check out almost any humorous birthday card aimed at the midthirties and beyond, and you'll find they're filled with any number of negative references about aging. Although we value old wine, old furniture, and old lace, this isn't the case when it comes to "old" people. Happily this is changing, in part due to an aging population of baby boomers who don't want and refuse to be shunned, and partly because we live in a consumer-oriented society where products, services, and legislation are driven by any large group that buys and votes.

But few grow up aspiring to be retired. And few desire to grow older. When these things happen—retirement and aging—they bring changes in how you're viewed by others and how you view yourself.

Having a healthy, happy retirement means defeating some of the strongly held social stereotypes about what it means to age or to be a retiree.

Defeating the Aging Stereotype

In large measure, having a healthy, happy retirement means defeating some of the strongly held social stereotypes about what it means to age or to be a retiree. Although some progress has been

The physical reality of aging, the experience of becoming middle aged or a senior citizen is subjective.

made in recent years, the older person is still often portrayed as either a creaky, white-haired, hearing-impaired semi-invalid eating a bowl of fiber-packed cereal, or the recipient of frequent chin tucks, face-lifts, and any number of other procedures to keep looking young at all costs. The evidence of your own eyes and experiences is probably enough to convince you that these stereotypes are not at all accurate. Studies show wide variation among older individuals on mental acuity, muscular strength, and every other characteristic. Simply put, evidence does not justify the automatic exclusion of older people from *any* activity.

Furthermore, if you choose, there's much you can do to combat the more obvious signs of aging, both physically and psychologically. On the physical side, find out more about diet and exercise. Consider joining a health club or hiring a physical trainer. Get regular medical checkups and make it a point to become medically savvy by reading, as well as having a dialogue with your physician. Attitudinally, learn to accept wrinkles, baldness, and graying hair as merit badges in living rather than stigmas. If you want, seek medical advice on how to cosmetically address some of these signs of aging—but remember those stereotypes.

Apart from anything else, *when* does "old" age begin? When does "middle" age begin, for that matter? (The MacArthur Foundation Research Network on Successful Midlife Development defines midlife as the years between ages thirty and seventy). But, despite the physical reality of aging, the experience of becoming middle aged or a senior citizen is usually quite *subjective*. For instance, the well known *midlife crisis* is defined not by its age parameters, but by the *personal* experiences of those in middle age. The experience is one not of age, but of perception. And remember, membership in the American Association of Retired Persons starts at age fifty, not somewhere in the midsixties or beyond.

The experience of mid- and older life centers around many things—people's images of themselves, their expectations of what they should have achieved by now, their perceptions about their relationships with others and how others see them (including their perceptions about how they're seen by *younger* people), and often their sense that time is slipping away. While older adulthood can be simply defined by age, the aging *experience* is a combination of both chronological age and subjective experience.

In short, don't buy into the image of the decrepit older person. You may have more experience, more gray hair, and perhaps more aches and pains than younger people, and you may no longer have a job. But that doesn't mean you lack wisdom, skill, or a strong sense of self.

CHANGING ROLES

1. Check off any of the following statements that best describes your feelings about your age and condition.

___Age is almost irrelevant to my life.   ___My life is effectively over.

___I've rarely felt more vigorous.   ___I'm not the person I used to be.

___I feel younger than my years.   ___I feel pretty ancient.

___I rarely give much thought to my age.   ___I often think or obsess about my age.

___I've slowed down, but not by much.   ___I'm saddened by my loss of vigor.

___I'm feeling older, but wiser.   ___I lament about my reduced capabilities.

___I'm excited about what's ahead.   ___I'm just waiting to die.

2. How are you feeling about your role in your family, community, and society? Check off any item that describes your feelings statement, and/or add others.

___a solid contributor   ___as good as ever   ___engaged and optimistic

___helpless   ___marginal   ___pretty capable

___quite vigorous   ___semieffective   ___superfluous

___unclear   ___insecure   ___totally useless

other: _____   _____

_____   _____

3. What do your answers to Questions 1 and 2 say about your general view of yourself and your life at this point?

_____

_____

_____

_____

4. How much of your self-image—the way you see and feel about yourself—is influenced or shaped by the way you think other people see you or what they feel about you?

_____

_____

_____

_____

_____

THINGS TO THINK ABOUT

- Do you have a healthy perspective on aging?
- Are you feeling optimistic about these changes in your life, or unclear or pessimistic? Did this entry help you to get in closer touch with your feelings?

Staying Well

One goal of life adjustment at any stage of life is wellness. Although at one time wellness simply meant a healthy body, it has now come to symbolize healthy body, mind, and spirit. Perhaps more important, it implies a *sense* of well-being. Based on the work of the MacArthur Foundation, wellness can be defined by six features:

- self-acceptance: a sense of personal satisfaction and a healthy self-image, regardless of the direction life may have taken

- purpose: a set of values and goals that gives direction and meaning to life

- environmental mastery: the ability to manage the tasks and demands of everyday life

- personal growth: a sense of accomplishment, personal competency, and continued development

- positive relationships: successful relationships that provide meaningful ties to the larger world

- autonomy: a sense of independence and self-determination

Combined with Erik Erikson's description of late adulthood as a time for self-satisfaction, personal appreciation, and acceptance, these six aspects of wellness define the tasks of later years, serving as a guide for your passage into retirement. Use this next journal entry to think about your sense of wellness and satisfaction.

WELLNESS

1. How satisfied are you with *yourself*?

_____

_____

_____

2. How satisfied are you with this period of your life?

_____

_____

_____

3. How do you feel about your accomplishments in life?

_____

_____

_____

4. Do you feel a sense of mastery and competency in your daily life?

_____

_____

5. Does your life have meaning at this time, and a sense of purpose or direction?

_____

_____

6. Do you feel in control of your life, and where it's going?

_____

_____

7. Are you satisfied with your current relationships? Do they provide meaningful ties to the world around you?

_____

_____

8. Assess and describe your current state of wellness.

_____

_____

_____

_____

_____

_____

THINGS TO THINK ABOUT

- Were these simple or difficult questions to answer?
- Did you find any of your answers difficult to accept? If so, why?
- What does this simple inventory tell you about yourself, your needs, and your desires at this time in your life? Should you return to this entry to complete it again in a few days or weeks?

Roles and Work

Making the transition from work to retirement involves sharp and abrupt changes in what's expected of you and in what you expect of yourself. Your role as a worker may be over, or at least reduced. But your role as a spouse or partner, parent, friend, and perhaps a child to your own parents doesn't come to a screeching halt, and neither do any of the other multiple roles you might play in your circle of family, friends, and community. These roles may change or in some way be affected by your retirement, and you may take on new roles over time.

Not everyone is able to let go of a particular role, take on a new role, or even recognize that they have more than one role. In fact, some people who are unable to let go of the role provided by their work find it difficult to enjoy retirement. Having given up the highly structured work role, they may have no clear direction about what to do next. After the first few weeks of freedom from strict schedules, they're faced with the problem of fashioning a new way of life. And, despite being told to be active, they find that there are few guideposts for restructuring the rest of their lives.

Your role as a worker may be over, or at least reduced. But your role as a spouse or partner, parent, friend, and perhaps a child to your own parents doesn't come to a screeching halt, and neither do any of the other multiple roles you might play in your circle of family, friends, and community.

Who Are You?

Perspective refers to an attitude or mental outlook. It means keeping things in proportion and seeing the *whole* picture, although your view may be limited by current circumstances. As you switch from one *primary* role (worker) to another (retiree), it's especially important to keep perspective.

There may be many things that cloud your vision, from financial worries to difficult-to-manage feelings and concerns about the future. Yet taking control and defining your future for yourself

—perhaps the greatest freedom of retirement—requires that you maintain or develop a new perspective. One way to keep perspective, and thus see things clearly, is to recognize that there's more to you than just your job and the role it provided. Besides being a retiree, you may *also* be a parent, a spouse, an artist, a volunteer, a gourmet, an expert on international affairs, a teacher, a grandparent, a writer, or an inventor.

WHO ELSE ARE YOU?

1. *Besides being a former worker, I'm . . .* _____

_____

_____

2. *My role as worker was important because . . .* _____

_____

_____

3. *My role as worker was unimportant because . . .* _____

_____

_____

4. *My most important three roles now are:* _____

a. _____

b. _____

c. _____

5. *My most interesting three roles now are:* _____

a. _____

b. _____

c. _____

6. *I'd like to further develop my current role as . . .* _____

_____

_____

7. *I'd like to create or further develop my future role as . . .* _____

_____

_____

8. Who are you? *I'm . . .* _____

_____

_____

THINGS TO THINK ABOUT

- Have you ever thought about your many different roles before? Have you thought about your other roles in addition to being a retiree?
- Were you able to define other roles for yourself besides worker or retiree? If not, do you need some help developing new roles or relationships?
- Is it liberating to consider your many roles, or do you have *too* many other roles? Do want to get rid of some roles in your retirement?

Acceptance and Self-Concept

Along with a reduction in income and power and a change in roles, retirement often brings a change in social status and perception. This not only involves the perception of others, but also self-concept.

Self-image is a reflection of how you *see* yourself. People with positive self-images think of themselves as reasonably effective and capable and as someone others would want to know. Personal identity reflects your sense of *who* you are or the way you view your role in the world and your relationships with others.

Your sense of identity is built upon the things you do, your impact on the world, and your perception of your value to others.

Self-image has a great deal to do with the value you place upon yourself, personal identity has more to do with the role(s) you see yourself playing.

People with a negative self-image often see themselves as incapable, and perhaps undesirable. People with poorly defined identities are often confused about what's important to them, their personal relationships, and the value of the things they do to others. Where self-image has a great deal to do with the value you place upon yourself, personal identity has more to do with the role(s) you see yourself playing. One is about your value to yourself, the other your value to others. Together they contribute to, and perhaps make up, your sense of self-esteem.

If your self-image and personal identity have been tied to your role as a worker, you may face difficulty accepting and adjusting to new or redefined roles. But, most likely, if you had a high degree of self-esteem, a strong self-image, and a well-defined sense of personal identity *before* retirement, things probably haven't changed too much. Here it's worth noting that experiences can weaken your sense of yourself, but they can also *strengthen* self-image, *boost* self-esteem, and help further develop and *solidify* personal identity.

Have things changed for you since approaching or entering retirement? If so, in which direction, or have you been left unchanged by retirement?

SELF-CONCEPT

1. Self-Esteem

a. Circle the number that most approximates your sense of self-regard: 1 equals feeling pretty lousy about yourself, and 5 equals feeling pretty great.

Low Self-Esteem			High Self-Esteem	
I really feel bad about myself			*I really feel good about myself*	
1	2	3	4	5

b. Explain your rating. How do you *feel* about yourself, and why?

_____

_____

_____

_____

c. Has your sense of self-esteem changed since retirement? If so, how?

_____

_____

_____

_____

2. Self-Image

a. How positive is your self-image? Again, circle whichever number comes closest to describing how you see yourself: 1 equals a negative self-image, where you feel pretty ineffective and incompetent, and 5 represents a positive self-image, where you feel capable and competent.

Negative Self-Image			Positive Self-Image	
I see myself as really ineffective			*I see myself as really effective*	
1	2	3	4	5

b. Explain your answer. How do you *see* yourself, and why?

_____

_____

_____

_____

c. Has your self-image changed since retirement? If so, how?

_____

_____

_____

3. Personal Identity

a. How clear is your sense of personal identity?

Confused and Uncertain Identity			Clear and Certain Identity	
I'm confused or uncertain about my roles			*I'm clear and certain about my roles*	
1	2	3	4	5

b. Explain your answer. In what ways do you experience confusion or clarity about who you are as a person, both in terms of identity and role?

_____

_____

_____

_____

c. Has your sense of personal identity changed since retirement? If so, how?

_____

_____

_____

_____

4. What *is* your overall self-concept? How do you generally see yourself?

_____

_____

_____

_____

5. How much has retirement affected your overall self-concept?

_____

_____

_____

_____

6. What's been the most difficult part of maintaining a healthy self-concept since approaching or entering retirement, and why?

_____

_____

_____

_____

7. How much of your self-concept is affected by the way other people see you?

_____

_____

_____

_____

8. How are you feeling as you complete this entry?

_____

_____

_____

_____

_____

THINGS TO THINK ABOUT

- How do you judge yourself? Strong or weak, effective or ineffective? Do you understand why you evaluate yourself this way? What sort of things diminish your self-image, and what sort of things strengthen it?
- How important is self-concept in building your life and moving forward? Can you succeed without a positive opinion of yourself? If not, how can you begin to build positive self-image?
- Do you let other people's opinions of you shape your self-concept too much, and if so is this a dynamic you want to change?

Enjoying Retirement

Along with the work ethic, our society has built a hidden message that too much leisure is undesirable. Many people are never able to overcome the message echoed in the common complaint of "being put out to pasture" or other implications of uselessness. Here, there are few role models from whom to learn and, for most of us, little chance to *ease* into the retirement mode; few companies permit workers to gradually taper off work until retirement. Indeed, for most retirees, it's a matter of going to work on Friday as usual, with no work and nowhere to go the following Monday, the first day of retirement.

Retirees who have lost their partners because of death or divorce are at a special disadvantage, as they lack an important source of support. This is especially true for women who, because they live longer than men and tend to marry husbands older than themselves, often find themselves widowed. On the other hand, women are more likely to have a strong network of friends and to be in close contact with other family members. But, whether male or female, it's difficult to be cut off from daily contact with coworkers. If you add to that facing retired life without a spouse or living by yourself, the loneliness multiplies.

It's especially important, then, to both enjoy the leisure that retirement allows and ensure you have a support network of people to whom you can turn for support, companionship, and with whom you can share your life. Use the final entry in this chapter to consider your own retirement and how to both maximize it and avoid some of the common pitfalls.

ADJUSTING TO RETIREMENT

1. What do you expect of yourself in retirement?

_____

_____

_____

_____

2. In general:

a. *With my added leisure time I will . . .* _____

_____

b. *To maintain and develop friendships I will . . .* _____

_____

c. *To keep my mind active I will . . .* _____

_____

d. *To keep physically active I will . . .* _____

_____

3. What do you think your family and friends expect of you as a retiree?

a. your spouse/partner: _____

_____

b. your children: _____

_____

c. your siblings: _____

_____

d. your parents: _____

_____

e. your friends: _____

_____

f. other important people in your life: _____

_____

4. Do you think there are serious conflicts in expectations between what you want from your retirement and what others expect? If so, what are they?

_____

_____

_____

_____

5. What can you do to reduce any potential conflicts or friction?

_____

_____

_____

_____

6. Can you think of any friends or acquaintances who've retired with seeming ease and grace? If so, who are they? Can you ask them about the secret of their retirement success?

_____

_____

_____

_____

7. What makes a successful retirement?

_____

_____

_____

_____

_____

Making Your Retirement Your Own

Studies show that most retirees are satisfied with retirement. Most adapt to the changes and find the benefits of not working. Despite the occasional horror story, most retirees keep busy and enjoy their lives. They do things around the house, they read, garden, play golf, join clubs, develop new interests, travel, and see more of their friends and relatives.

Just as you made it through life's other transitions—from adolescence to adulthood, from single to married life, from childhood to parenthood—you'll make it through the retirement transition, too, especially if you give some thought and apply some planning to the challenges. When you retire your role *does* change. You'll have very little value to your former employer or the workforce, and your relationships with your spouse or partner, children, relatives, and friends will be altered. You can govern that change to a large degree if you're willing to apply some clear thinking and straight talking. You'll have to reject society's prevailing thinking about aging. You'll have to follow your own dictates, regardless of what others might say or think, and you'll have to pursue new interests and new ways of looking at things.

6

Destination:

DISCOVERING ALL

YOU CAN DO

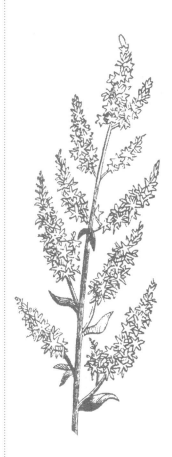

MIRIAM

I'm in my midseventies now, and I went to college at a time when few women did. My father thought that was achievement enough and got in the way of my plans for law school. I became a social worker instead, and an activist for feminist causes. I was a member of the League of Women Voters and the American Association of University Women. I marched for passage of the Equal Rights Amendment and took an active role in local civic affairs. But only after my retirement was I able to fulfill my passion for the law. I'm now a special advocate in the juvenile court, doing investigations for the judges and monitoring services available to children in foster care. I report to the judges and make recommendations for legal action. It's interesting and rewarding volunteer work, and it feels great to finally sit in the courtroom and play an official role for which I'm recognized.

ONE OF THE greatest challenges in retirement is getting involved in activities, interests, and relationships that will prove satisfying over the long-term. But, for many people that's easier said than done.

95

Some retirees literally hit the deck running. They jump into community activities, sports, or other personal interests they've been waiting to pursue for many years. But many other retirees are shy about seeking outside activities at all, or getting involved with a new community or people. Some wonder who would want them to get involved anyway, and still others have led closed lives and don't know *how* to get involved. Still other retirees feel they can't afford to do anything new or different, and some who may be used to measuring everything financially may think that if a new activity doesn't produce income, it's not worth pursuing.

An amazing array of learning and interactional opportunities exist for the retired person who's open to them. Taking advantage of such opportunities can allow you to meet your own needs, as well as using your skills and interests to help others.

Fear of being a beginner also inhibits many. Yet, an amazing array of learning and interactional opportunities exist for the retired person who's open to them. These range from teaching already developed skills to others as a mentor to volunteering, learning new skills, and pursuing personal interests. Taking advantage of such opportunities can allow you to meet your own needs, as well as using your skills and interests to help others. It also allows you to open up a whole new world of interests and skills. There are retired bankers who sculpt and bakers who paint, engineers who become photographers, dentists who work as museum lecturers, barbers who consult on small businesses, and secretaries who become authorities on Irish music. These are people who become deeply involved in developing new skills and enriching their own lives and the lives of others and who find affirmation, excitement, and challenge in learning and mastering new skills.

An important first step to deciding how to begin is to look deep within your own head and heart.

WHAT DO YOU WANT TO BE WHEN YOU GROW UP?

1. What do you want to accomplish in the next ten years?

_____

_____

_____

2. What skills do you most want to develop?

_____

_____

_____

3. What have you always wanted to do but never allowed yourself to do because it was too expensive, reckless, or likely to be frowned upon by others?

_____

_____

_____

4. Use these sentence starts to think about the possibilities for your life.

a. *If I could live my life over, I would . . .* _____

_____

b. *If a newspaper were to run an article about what I did in the first ten years of my retirement, I hope it would say . . .* _____

_____

c. *I would most like to learn to . . .* _____

_____

5. What most stops you from taking the plunge into developing these other interests and skills?

_____

_____

_____

- Sometimes choice can be overwhelming. Is it liberating to think about all the things you can or might do, or frightening?
- It's easy to write about possibilities, but hard to turn them into realities. Were you just writing about possibilities, or were you thinking about actually turning them into reality?

Eight More Lives

Just as cats have nine lives, so do people. Perhaps you're feeling as though one of those lives ended when you retired; but that leaves you with eight more. Your other eight figurative lives can be other roles you play or interests you have in your *current* life, or other lives you'd like to live in your *future*.

Perhaps you are:	*Perhaps you'd* like *to:*
a parent	get involved in a sport
a musician	return to school
an athlete	become a writer
a partner in a marriage	develop a whole new career
a volunteer in the community	become a consultant to businesses
an artist	lecture or write a book on retirement
an avid hobbyist	build a small business

Use the next journal entry to think about those other eight lives, or what they *might* be. Use the entry to not only keep perspective on who you are, but also to seriously consider other options for future lives and interests that can realistically develop for you if you choose to pursue them. Thinking about who you are and who you'd like to be is not only an important way to keep perspective, but also a useful way to think about your future and other directions you might like to take.

YOUR OTHER EIGHT LIVES

1. First give a name to the life that just ended. *My life as* . . . _____

_____

2. Who else are you? List eight other lives in your *current* life.

a. _____   e. _____

b. _____   f. _____

c. _____   g. _____

d. _____   h. _____

3. Of these, which ones are the most satisfying?

_____

_____

_____

_____

_____

4. Which other present lives would you like to develop further?

_____

_____

_____

_____

_____

5. What prevents you from developing these other current lives further?

_____

_____

_____

_____

_____

6. Who else would you like to be? List eight other possible *future* lives.

a. _____   e. _____

b. _____   f. _____

c. _____   g. _____

d. _____   h. _____

7. Which of these future lives can be lived part of the time, and which require a full-time commitment?

_____

_____

_____

_____

8. Which future life would you most like to live right now?

_____

9. What's stopping you from living that life now?

_____

_____

_____

_____

THINGS TO THINK ABOUT

- Is your current life richer than you previously imagined? Are your future interest and desires realistic? If not, what do you need to do to make them realistic?
- Was it difficult to think of eight other present lives or eight future lives? If it was, why? What limits your ability to consider other aspects of your current life or imagine other futures for yourself?

The Courage to Begin Again

The American businessman, writer, and printer Elbert Hubbard said, "There is no failure except in no longer trying." But for many, it seems just too frightening to start over again, too disempowering to become a beginner once more, too humiliating to have to ask questions and get help, or just too intimidating to be in a classroom or a learning environment. For some people, past learning experiences have been difficult and frustrating, and they've spent a lifetime avoiding situations where they might once again experience a sense of failure or incompetence.

In some cases, it may mean applying your skills and your lifetime of experiences as an older adult to go *back* into an environment that you once learned to fear—not only facing the challenge and learning a new skill, but *overcoming* a past fear and becoming a stronger person. For others, it may mean accepting the humility of not being the teacher, and instead becoming the student. In still other cases, it may not mean going into a classroom or formal learning environment at all, but may be a *field* learning experience, like learning to paint, studying wild birds, learning to play golf, or volunteering at a local food pantry.

Not everyone is intimidated by a new challenge or prevented from doing something they really want to do. But many are, and for many different reasons. The goal, though, is to first recognize those things that might prevent you from taking a challenge and stretching yourself in new directions, and then overcoming those obstacles so you can become the person you've always wanted to be and now *can* become.

For some people, past learning experiences have been difficult and frustrating, and they've spent a lifetime avoiding situations where they might once again experience a sense of failure or incompetence.

WHAT DO YOU FEAR?

"The only thing we have to fear is fear itself."
—FRANKLIN D. ROOSEVELT

1. What most prevents you from taking up new challenges? Check all that apply and/or add other obstructions.

___ actively discouraged by others   ___ lack of interest

___ economic costs   ___ lack of personal energy

___ expectation of quitting anyway   ___ not enough personal energy

___ fear of failure   ___ see little point

___ fear of humiliation   ___ shyness

___ lack of encouragement from others   ___ too much trouble

other: _____   _____

_____   _____

_____   _____

_____   _____

2. What fears or personal concerns most prevent you from putting yourself into a new learning situation? Again, check any relevant answer and/or add more.

___ being in a *learning* situation   ___ having to ask for help

___ being in *new* situations   ___ having to open up to people

___ feeling incompetent   ___ meeting new people

___ feeling like a novice   ___ possibility of failure

other: _____   _____

_____   _____

_____   _____

_____   _____

3. Look back at your answers to Questions 1 and 2. What does your pattern of answers tell you?

_____

_____

_____

_____

4. Are you someone who normally overcomes all obstacles or gives in to them without pushing on?

_____

_____

_____

_____

a. Do you rationalize reasons for not pushing yourself further?

_____

_____

b. Do you let your fears and your worries stop you?

_____

_____

5. How important is it to you to pursue the things you're interested in, and overcome barriers?

_____

_____

_____

_____

_____

6. If you aren't able to overcome whatever reservations and concerns you might have about new undertakings, how might this affect your retirement?

_____

_____

_____

_____

_____

THINGS TO THINK ABOUT

- Even if you're someone who usually doesn't let things stand in your way, are there other areas in your life where you feel inhibited, such as new relationships or accepting new responsibilities?
- Are you comfortable with who you are in this area, or do you feel that it's important to work to overcome your own fears and inhibitions?

Meet the Enemy: Isolation

One of the advantages in being open to opportunities for growth is the chance to get out there and meet and mix with new people. But for many retired people and retired couples, the greatest enemy is isolation.

Of course, you'll need quiet time for reading, gardening, and other solitary pursuits, and, if you're part of a couple, you'll need time for yourselves and your intimate life together. But unless you're going to retire from the *world* and not just your job, you'll also need to remain connected to people already in your life as well as develop new relationships. Your life will change over the years ahead, and so will your relationship needs. People close to you now are not likely to always be in your life. Some may move away as part of their own retirement plans, others may become infirmed, and still others will pass away. Relationships become important, then, not just to meet current social needs, but as part of your future, ensuring that retirement doesn't now or eventually isolate you from the world.

In addition to meeting the plain need for friendship and socializing, interacting with other people keeps you alive to new ideas and new experiences and allows you the opportunity to engage in group activities and adventures that are not otherwise available to you.

In many ways, we're defined and define ourselves *by* our relationships. How you see yourself is quite likely affected deeply by your relationships—the more positive, gratifying, and supportive relationships you've had, the more likely you are to feel good about yourself. This isn't to say that good relationships are the be-all and end-all to self-image, but they're certainly a powerful start. The same is true now as you near or enter your retirement, and the same will be true throughout your retirement. Too many retirees depend on their work relationships and become isolated after leaving their jobs, or begin to lose their contacts with the world outside until they eventually wind up lonely, isolated, and insulated from all the opportunities offered to them by their retirement.

How you see yourself is quite likely affected deeply by your relationships—the more positive, gratifying, and supportive relationships you've had, the more likely you are to feel good about yourself.

CONNECTIONS

1. Are relationships an important part of your life?

_____

_____

2. Do you see relationships as an increasingly important aspect of your retirement?

_____

_____

3. Are you content with just keeping the relationships you currently have, or do you feel you need to develop new relationships as well?

_____

_____

_____

_____

4. Is it frightening or anxiety provoking to think of life alone, if not now then in the future?

_____

_____

_____

_____

5. Are you open and outgoing, or do you tend to isolate yourself?

_____

_____

_____

_____

6. What will retirement be like without relationships with others?

_____

_____

_____

_____

7. What do you most need to do to keep your relationships alive and active?

_____

_____

_____

_____

8. What most prevents you from actively developing existing relationships or seeking new ones?

_____

_____

_____

_____

_____

Passion, Place, People, and Posterity

Much of the well-meaning advice given to the new, or soon-to-be, retirees is along the lines of "keep busy." That's true as far as it goes, and it's certainly part of what's being said right here in this chapter. Probably *any* activity at all will help carry out that prescription to keep busy, from weeding the garden to visiting friends. But to find activities that are *meaningful* is quite another task, and many retirees find that looking for fulfilling ways to spend their time is onerous. To some, it's almost like seeking a new job.

The fact is that even if it keeps you *busy* not every activity is best suited for *you*. Playing dominoes, going to stock-car races, attending the opera, or joining an investment club are activities that will be exciting to some and boring to others. And if you keep busy at something that isn't a good fit for you, then you likely won't keep it up for very long. Dust will start to cover your domino tiles, and you'll become less and less motivated to drag yourself to the stock-car races. So it's crucial to find a passionate, personal connection, as well as variety and balance in your pursuits. Those are higher and tougher goals than just keeping busy, but worth the effort.

As you think about the activities and relationships in your retirement, consider the four P's:

- Passion: doing what you love to do

- Place: finding an environment where you can utilize your talents and which supports your creativity

- People: engaging in meaningful and supportive relationships

- Posterity: remembering what you wish to leave behind in your relationships, in your activities, and in your life

Finding a Sense of Balance

When we consider well-being, we think in terms of healthy body, healthy mind, and healthy spiritual self. Here, healthy body requires little further explanation. Mental health requires a little more explanation, referring to emotions and thoughts that help and are satisfying rather than hindering you or causing undue distress. And spiritual health is still more complicated.

Your spiritual beliefs refer to the sense of meaning you derive from your life and your world or the meaning you inject into the world.

In this context, *spirit* involves neither a belief in ghosts nor religion. Instead, the word is used in much the same way as we refer to old school spirit, or the spirit of an idea. Your spiritual beliefs refer to the sense of meaning you derive from your life and your world or the meaning you inject into the world. Used this way, spirit is the animating or the motivating factor that drives us on. For some people, spiritual life is more connected to their *sense* of well-being than any other part of this trinity of body, mind, and spirit.

As you think about and plan for your retirement, try to think in terms of balancing body, mind, and spirit. This means, for instance, balancing social, solitary, and physical activities for a complete life. You may fill your social quota by spending time with your spouse or family, with visits to friends, or in volunteer work at a local hospital. But a balanced life will also likely require time invested in a solitary pursuit like reading, hiking, thinking, or journaling. Taking care of your health might mean watching your diet, a daily workout routine, or morning yoga, but it can also be coupled with either a *solitary* activity like hiking alone into the woods or a *social* biking trip with your spouse or friends. The point is to think of your whole self—body, mind, and spirit—as both an individual *and* a social creature.

Do your proposed activities and relationships provide the needed variety? The range of available activities is, of course, enormous. But it will be narrowed by circumstances. Financial constraints, for instance, where you simply can't afford a particular activity, or physical or health problems that limit your ability to engage in certain activities. Or perhaps your family, friends, and acquaintances don't enjoy the same activities as you. Equally to the point, do your activities and relationships interest you? If they don't, it's like eating a balanced meal that's full of nutrition but lacking flavor. For these and other reasons, only *you* can select and balance the activities, relationships, and lifestyle that fit your particular retirement.

Helping Yourself by Helping Others

Social service and volunteerism aren't for everyone. But many people who've spent a lifetime working for business, industry, or themselves feel a need to work with others but have never found the time. This pursuit often gets lost somewhere in the years when they were supporting themselves and their families. A large number of retirees, though, find special pride and satisfaction in giving service because they *want* to. They're not obligated to do so by contract or even conscience but because they feel another person's need is greater than their own.

In some cases, retired people return to college and go on to become teachers and social workers. But in more cases, retirees can fill a personal need that has often gone unfulfilled for a lifetime by returning to the community as a volunteer of some kind. It's not at all unusual to find retired men and women filling various volunteer roles in hospitals, soup kitchens, adult reading literacy programs, elementary and high schools, shelters, Red Cross offices, and other social service agencies, or volunteering their services as a "big brother" or "big sister." Equally, you'll find retirees serving on the boards of their local libraries or other local social and human service organizations or working with local leisure services as coaches and officials for little league and other kids' sports activities.

As a volunteer, you have several advantages. You have time available during the day when younger volunteers are making a living. No longer concerned with advancing your career, you can be less concerned with making business contacts or appearing important. Time and experience have given you objectivity and the good judgment lacking in many younger people.

All these things serve to enrich the life of the retiree and the community. This work provides meaning, status, recognition, respect, and a sense of connection, and in many ways offers the very balance that links body, mind, and spirit. Volunteer work is deeply personal, social, and often involves some level of physical activity. And there's a lot to be said for keeping busy by helping others. For one thing, there's an enormous need and, further,

Retirees can fill a personal need that has often gone unfulfilled for a lifetime by returning to the community as a volunteer of some kind.

such service can be an antidote for the isolation that's so devastating to many retirees.

Like everything else in your retirement, if you choose to spend some of your time as a volunteer, your choice of service should meet *your* needs as well as the needs of your community. In other words, *you* should choose. Use the next journal entry to think about whether volunteer service is an avenue to pursue. If you know already that volunteer work isn't for you right now, for any reason, skip the entry. You can always come back to it if you decide to think about volunteerism at a later time. If you're not sure and just want to explore the idea of volunteer work, use the entry to explore your ideas and questions. If you're ready to start volunteering your time, the entry offers a useful way to think through what you want do, with what type of population, and how much time you want to commit.

Volunteer work is deeply personal, social, and often involves some level of physical activity. And there's a lot to be said for keeping busy by helping others.

GIVING YOUR TIME

1. *Do* you want to volunteer your time? Why or why not? If not, skip this entry and come back to it if you later decide that you want to think further about volunteer work.

_____

_____

_____

_____

2. When did you first think about becoming a volunteer?

_____

_____

_____

_____

3. Have you been a volunteer before? If so, what was the experience like?

_____

_____

_____

_____

4. What sort of things have held you back from volunteering in the past?

_____

_____

_____

_____

5. What sort of things might hold you back now?

_____

_____

_____

_____

6. What sort of personal gains do you think you might acquire from serving as a volunteer?

_____

_____

_____

_____

7. In what ways might the community benefit from your service as a volunteer?

_____

_____

_____

_____

8. What sort of volunteer work do you want to do?

_____

_____

_____

_____

THINGS TO THINK ABOUT

- Do you have a sense of whether volunteer work is something you want to do?
- What most concerns you about volunteer work at this time in your life? If you have mixed feelings about being a volunteer, is there a way to test out the waters? Do you know anyone you can talk to about volunteer work?
- Do you think being a volunteer will enrich your life? If so, how?

Connecting the Dots

As you reach the end of this chapter, you've thought and written about expanding and developing your life so that it incorporates activities, relationships, and balance. As a retiree, you have an unusual and well-deserved opportunity to build a rich and diverse life that includes solitary and deeply personal activities, social interactions and the deepening of relationships, and volunteerism and community involvement. In fact, your retirement is an incredibly *fertile* period in life, offering opportunities for personal growth, reflection, involvement, and self-gratification not fully available to those who still work, precisely *because* they still work.

We all age. But those with a healthy mental outlook and an active lifestyle teach their bodies to age more gracefully. Keeping the mind and body active, experts say, contributes to physical, emotional, and spiritual well-being. In other words, the common

Retirement is an incredibly fertile period in life, offering opportunities for personal growth, reflection, involvement, and self-gratification not fully available to those who still work, precisely because they still work.

refrain, "You're only as old as you think you are," has a scientific basis. And attitudes about aging are learned. As one senior put it, "People don't grow old. But when they stop growing, they become old."

Don't stop growing. Work at opening yourself up to new experiences. Try to be happier and more relaxed. Stay involved. Let go of long simmering resentments or old embarrassments, and instead embrace the opportunities that surround you. Try to get as much out of life as you can. Spend time doing things you personally find rewarding. And if doing so not only helps you but others as well, then so much the better.

In this chapter, you've barely scratched the surface, as there are as many possible activities as your mind can devise and more people to connect with than you could reach in a dozen lifetimes. The point is, now is the time to begin thinking about the kinds of things you're interested in doing and where and how to use your skills and interests. If you still find yourself feeling bored, disconnected, or useless, then perhaps you're looking with the wrong eyes or in the wrong places. It's time now for you to begin connecting the dots.

7

Destination:
GETTING STRAIGHT
ABOUT MONEY

RON

Holly and I wanted to stretch our small retirement income to the fullest. We thought about what we wanted to do as retirees, and it was as little as possible, other than be together, do some traveling, and share our hobby of landscape painting. So we moved to a Mexican border town and bought a condominium at a fraction of what it would cost in the United States, leaving enough for our other expenses. We regularly travel across the border to see our friends and family and do some shopping, but we mostly stay in Mexico, where the cost of living is low and the opportunities to paint nature are endless.

SARAH

As a widowed homemaker, I get by on little more than my Social Security check and some gifts from my kids. But I live in a mobile home in a blue-collar neighborhood where the costs are low, and I enjoy good health, family visits, and volunteering at my church. You need money to retire, but you need absorbing activities even more. I never expected to be rich in anything but friends, family, and things to do. And I was right.

BLANCA

Jorge and I ran a small chain of beauty parlors and poured money into our retirement for twenty-five years. A pretty good income and years of saving allow us to live very comfortably in our retirement. We have a large home on a golf course, travel a lot, and indulge in our passion for vintage cars. We were never poor, but we probably live better now than when we worked. It was a conscious choice, and we're happy we made it. This is the payoff for all those years of overtime and weekend work, for time away from home, for scrimping when we could've been living it up. We're both savers, but we both planned on doing our spending when we were most free to enjoy it.

WHATEVER YOUR AGE, one of the most common fears is that of not having enough money. For those who grew up during the Depression era, that dread is heightened. But for many, the thought of sliding into poverty or insolvency is never too distant. When you see a homeless person, when you recall a poor family from your youth (perhaps even your own), and, in fact, when you retire and say goodbye to a regular paycheck, those old fears may come cascading back.

Consider carefully all the motivational forces in your life at this time, not just money alone.

There are shelves and shelves of excellent books, tapes, and other resources that tell you how to financially plan for your retirement, develop a household budget, invest and grow your money, and create new sources of income. They tell how to balance risk and reward, beat inflation, and enjoy the good life. *The Healing Journey Through Retirement* is not a financial planner, and the goals of planning, investing, and stretching your money and financial resources are way beyond the scope and intention of this book. Instead, it is the purpose of this chapter to help you think about and understand your relationship with money and what it means to you.

We're always in the position of having to make choices. Despite the difficulty of managing life with a reduced income, consider carefully *all* the motivational forces in your life at this time, not just money alone. Take the time to think carefully about the decisions you make, the things that you allow to shape those decisions, and the way you want to live your life.

The Meaning of Money

Money means vastly different things to different people. For some, money is just a means to an end; the entire reason to earn money is so you can buy the things you need or want. For others, money *is* the end, representing security and filling an emotional need. In some cases, money is a means to earn still more money, and in still other cases, money is a means for gaining control over a dog-eat-dog world. For some, money buys far more than just basic needs and is a measure of power. And money is the thing that fuels many of the accomplishments of humankind.

There's an old Jack Benny routine that exemplified his stage relationship with money. In it, he's approached by a mugger who demands, "Your money or your life." Benny responds with silence, and the mugger repeats, "Your money or your life." Again, the mugger is greeted with silence. Agitated now, the mugger says, "I said 'Your money or your life.'" This time Jack Benny answers him, "Wait a minute. I'm thinking."

What's your relationship with money? Like it or not, money is something that people have an important relationship with. Is it a godsend, or the root of all evil? Is it something that merely enhances your life, or is it something you can't live without?

THE COLOR OF MONEY

1. *Money is important in my life because it . . .*

___ allows me the freedom to do what I want.

___ allows me to take control of my own future.

___ allows me to do things for other people.

___ allows me to show my love and affection for the people in my life.

___ allows me to take care of myself without depending on handouts.

___ gives me a measure of control over family members.

___ helps me measure how well I'm doing versus my friends and acquaintances.

___ is a major source of self-esteem.

___ provides a sense of security.

___ reflects how society values my contribution.

___ wins me respect from friends and acquaintances.

other: _____

other: _____

other: _____

2. How much does money control your life?

_____

_____

_____

_____

3. Does money control your life more than you'd like it to? In what ways *does* money control or affect your life?

_____

_____

_____

_____

4. Does a fear of not having money prevent you from living your life more fully?

_____

_____

_____

_____

_____

5. Can you live a rewarding and satisfying life, even on a reduced income?

_____

_____

_____

_____

6. What role does money play in your life? *Money is . . .* _____

_____

_____

_____

_____

THINGS TO THINK ABOUT

- What does money represent in your life? A necessary means to an end, or an end in and of itself? Either way, does your attitude toward money contribute to your ability to lead an emotional healthy life or hold you back?
- Do you need to rethink your relationship with money?
- Is money the only thing holding you back from the sort of life you want to lead?

All in the Family

Although money is important to many people, it's more important to take charge of your *attitude* toward money. This is doubly true in retirement, when the flow of money usually changes along with the ways in which it's spent. How much you need depends to a very large extent on how much you *think* you need. Two people, even in the same household, can have identical needs and income, yet one will feel secure while the other suffers from enormous anxiety about money.

How much you need depends to a very large extent on how much you think *you need.*

In a marriage or other committed relationship, retirement actively affects both parties, directly or indirectly. If one partner is spending money like it's going out of style, the other partner may become worried or concerned. Conversely, if one party is holding on to money and reluctant to spend it under any circumstances, it may become stressful or uncomfortable for the other person in the relationship. Under the best of circumstances, both partners feel the same way and share the same attitude toward money.

Is your financial style focused on current or future needs? Is it consistent with being retired and on a reduced income, or are you still spending money as though you were still working? Does your money style make sense for you and for your family?

The next journal entry is intended for people in a marriage or other committed relationship. If this isn't you, then pass on the entry. But consider looking it over anyway, as it may help you to think a little further about your relationship with and style of handling money.

LIVING TOGETHER WITH MONEY

1. Answer each question by checking off one of the answers to the right of the question.

My spouse/partner and I . . .	Yes	No	Sometimes
agree about the role and importance of money in our lives	___	___	___
agree to share our financial situation with our children	___	___	___
are both comfortable with the way we each spend money	___	___	___
are both knowledgeable about our financial situation	___	___	___
argue over money matters	___	___	___
avoid using money as a way to get power or control	___	___	___
both know where our important financial records are kept	___	___	___
both practice disciplined saving	___	___	___
consult one another before spending any significant sums	___	___	___
differ in our opinion of how much retirement income we'll need	___	___	___
freely discuss our financial goals	___	___	___
share financial tasks such as budgeting and paying bills	___	___	___

2. Check off only those items that are accurate. *My spouse and I have . . .*

___ complete financial records (income, expenses, receipts, etc.)

___ a reliable financial advisor

___ a reserve of six months' income to see us through emergencies

___ a safe place for credit cards and other valuable documents

___ a set of written instructions in case of death or disability

___ a written yearly financial plan

___ updated wills

3. *My spouse's attitude toward money is . . .* _____

_____

4. Look at your answers. Is there a pattern of some kind? Are you and your spouse on the same page when it comes to money and your finances?

_____

_____

_____

_____

5. Do you share enough financial information with your spouse? If not, what gets in the way?

_____

_____

_____

_____

6. Are there issues and communication problems that you ought to work out with your spouse? If so, what are they?

_____

_____

_____

_____

THINGS TO THINK ABOUT

- Are your family's finances a one-person show or a joint responsibility? Is this arrangement working well? Could it become a problem in the *future*?
- Do you and your spouse or partner need to improve your communication around financial issues? Should you keep better financial records or share more information?
- Are both you and your spouse satisfied with the way you deal with money? Have you and your spouse had problems in the past over differences in attitude toward and handling of money?

Planning How to Spend Money

The way people approach money in retirement can vary enormously. Some retirees chose fairly frugal lifestyles in order to afford occasional indulgences like exotic trips. For others, having a top-drawer lifestyle during each day of retirement makes an important statement that's at the heart of who they are. Others are glad just to be free of work and still have enough to make ends meet.

Financial experts often say retirees need 60–80% of their final working income available during retirement if they're to maintain anything approaching their former lifestyle. But, obviously, what's just getting by to some is luxury living to others. And living well doesn't always depend on having more money.

Rarely do we analyze our true needs and habits. Just as we plan for physical fitness though, we must plan for fiscal fitness. Coming up with such a plan and then sticking to it can take willpower and determination. We all have ingrained habits about how we use money, what degree of satisfaction we derive from it, and how much risk we're willing to take with our money.

Financially speaking, retirement can be a wall: You probably won't have as much money as you used to and that can stop you short. But it also can be a door: Maybe you don't need as much money as you used to, and perhaps you can walk through that door to a different way of living. In retirement, some of your expenses may be lower, others higher. Your mortgage may be paid off or may at least be at a relatively low interest rate. You may no longer have to worry about a working wardrobe, the costs of a daily commute, and daily lunches. And maybe you'll no longer need to keep up appearances by having a late-model car or a state-of-the-art cell phone or laptop computer.

On the other hand, leisure activity and travel may take a bigger chunk of your disposable income. You may spend more on your

Financial experts often say retirees need 60–80% of their final working income available during retirement if they're to maintain anything approaching their former lifestyle.

grandkids. Health care costs are likely to increase. Without planning, you may be spending in a thoughtless, wasteful way. In fact, in light of your specific situation as a retired person, the *major* reason to consider your relationship with money right now is so that you can continue to live a meaningful, satisfying, and productive life even without the level of income you formerly had or feel you must regain. But, beyond putting money in its place, it's important for you to be considering how to manage financial resources that have now become scarce. This usually means a financial plan of some kind.

By this point, as you near or have entered retirement, you certainly should have given thought to, developed, and be using some sort of financial plan to help project present and future income and expenses. If you haven't, then you're either financially independent, floating along okay even with reduced resources, or you're really struggling with money, in which case you need to get some outside help at once. There are *many* resources that can help you to analyze and develop financial plans and budgets.

If you *are* struggling with financial pressures and realities, all the thinking, discussion, and self-exploration in the world will do little to alleviate the situation unless you're seriously prepared to significantly alter your lifestyle (and the lifestyle of your family, if you're married). Otherwise, you may need some concrete outside help. There are many professionally written self-help books and tapes available, as well as accountants and financial counselors who can help you analyze your situation and plan very carefully. One thing to avoid is leaning on credit too heavily, or leaning on the wrong kind of credit. Running up credit cards bills, for instance, may help today, but can exhaust or wipe you out later.

Use the next journal entry as a guide to help shape your thoughts about your financial situation, how you see and are dealing with it, and whether or not you need to get some more help and direction.

If you are struggling with financial pressures and realities, all the thinking, discussion, and self-exploration in the world will do little to alleviate the situation unless you're seriously prepared to significantly alter your lifestyle (and the lifestyle of your family, if you're married).

A FRANK LOOK AT MONEY

1. Are you concerned about your expenses and your level of income?

_____

_____

_____

_____

2. Have you discussed these issues with anyone else? If so, who and what sort of response have they had? If you haven't, why not?

_____

_____

_____

_____

_____

3. If you have financial concerns, are there lifestyle changes you can make to cut back on or eliminate expenses? If so, what are they?

_____

_____

_____

_____

_____

4. Can you make changes that will affect parts of your lifestyle, but not in any significant way? For instance, would you consider a smaller home, a different or only one car, eating out less often, giving up a club membership, or selling off some assets?

_____

_____

_____

_____

5. Are there areas of your life in which you cannot or will not cut back expenses? If so, describe them and why you can't or won't make changes?

_____

_____

_____

_____

6. Are you fearful that cutting back expenses will:

___ be an admission of failure ___ be a blow to your self-esteem

___ be the beginning of a downslide ___ cause friends to spurn you

___ damage your pride ___ make you look bad

___ significantly reduce your quality of life ___ set you apart from your friends

___ let down your spouse and family members ___ worry your spouse and family members

other: _____ _____

_____ _____

_____ _____

7. What might happen if you *don't* cut back expenses?

_____

_____

_____

_____

8. What's worse, the trade-offs you identified in Question 6 or the consequences of *not* cutting back or finding some other solution?

_____

_____

_____

_____

9. How will cutting back or *not* cutting back expenses affect other important people in your life, such as a spouse or children?

_____

_____

_____

_____

_____

THINGS TO THINK ABOUT

- If married or in a committed relationship, have you and your spouse discussed these issues and options openly and fully?
- Can you develop a financial plan on your own, or do you need some outside help? Is it difficult for you to ask for help?
- Do you typically share your thoughts and concerns with others, or do you tend to keep things inside? Do you generally listen to or disregard the opinions of others? Whichever pattern most describes you, is it the best or most appropriate way to deal with this situation?

Money: The Bottom Line

Your income will most likely decrease when you retire. Thus, it becomes more important than ever to understand what money means to you. You'll need to sort out your fiscal priorities, to break the code of family silence, if there is one about money, and to figure out ways to come to grips with your money attitudes so you can maximize your retirement pleasure. If you've always had an easygoing attitude about money, that probably won't significantly change. If you've always fretted over every dime, that anxiety may not disappear overnight.

It is important to understand what money means to you because your income will most likely decrease when you retire.

It is important to understand what money means to you because your income will most likely decrease when you retire.

Putting Money in Its Place

How much is money, your concern about it, and your drive to not be without it, affecting your life at this time, and how much will it affect your retirement in the future? Is it shaping your life, as though it was the most important thing in your life, and *is* it the most important thing? Or are there other, more important, driving forces in your life? More to the point, are you clear about how to live your life with or without money? Use the last journal entry in this chapter to think about how to best tuck money into a healthy place in your life.

A HEALTHY APPRECIATION

1. What constitutes a healthy appreciation for money?

___ an understanding of your attitude toward money

___ earning and having money without condemning or worshiping it

___ refusing to sacrifice moral or ethical standards for money

___ the ability to use money to improve your life and the lives of those around you

___ the ability to use money without being used by it

___ using money to provide for pleasure as well as necessities

other: _____

_____

_____

2. Conversely, what constitutes an unhealthy attitude or relationship with money?

_____

_____

_____

_____

3. How has your attitude toward or relationship with money shaped and affected your life until now?

_____

_____

_____

_____

4. Has that relationship changed much since nearing or entering retirement?

_____

_____

_____

_____

5. How has your attitude and appreciation for money affected the life of your spouse and children, if you're married?

_____

_____

_____

_____

6. What's the most important thing you've learned about money since your retirement?

_____

_____

_____

_____

7. What has money taught you about yourself?

_____

_____

_____

_____

THINGS TO THINK ABOUT

- Do you need to make changes in your relationship with or attitude about money? Are you in control of the money in your life, or is it in control of you?
- Do you believe that money should be an important and useful supplement to your life, or the driving force? Do you have some other beliefs about money and the role it should play in your life?
- Has money helped you achieve your most meaningful goals, or can these be accomplished without having any money at all? Has money stood in the way of accomplishing meaningful personal goals?

8

Destination:

ANOTHER JOB OR BUSINESS

BUD

I always had a lot of energy and was always a hard worker. A couple of years before my planned retirement, my wife died. As I got closer and closer to being retired, I realized I couldn't stand the thought of being alone and doing nothing all day long after I quit work. So while I was still making good money, I invested several thousand dollars in the equipment and training I needed to become a one-man carpet and upholstery cleaning business. I printed up some business cards, took out a small ad, and pretty soon I had as much work as I wanted. By the time I retired from my "real" job—getting the benefit of not only a pension, but also of being my own boss— I'd already developed the next step in my life. My small business is no Fortune 500 company, but it keeps me as busy as I want to be, brings in a little extra money, and, maybe most important, keeps me in contact with people all day.

MANY RETIREES FIND that something is lacking in retirement and come to feel that they can compensate for this lack by getting back in the workforce, at least partially. Even if they don't need to work for financial reasons, they may wish to return to a work environment for psychological purposes. Too much leisure can be as deadly as too much stress. As George Bernard Shaw put it, "The secret of being miserable is to have the leisure to bother about whether you are happy or not."

Today's retirees are leaving their careers earlier, healthier, and more active than their predecessors. When retirees return to the job market, they generally want lower stress, flexible hours, work that they enjoy, and a sense that they're making a difference. And they're finding myriad opportunities, from returning to the workforce in another role to volunteering. In fact, many retirees do their best and hardest work following their retirement and subsequent return to work.

Too much leisure can be as deadly as too much stress.

If you think you'll have trouble keeping busy after you retire, need to supplement your income, have a marketable skill or interest, and/or you're a "people person" who fears loneliness in retirement, then finding a new job of some kind or buying or starting a small business may be worth considering.

Do You Want to Give Up Your Leisure?

There are a number of reasons why you might want to forfeit some or all of your retirement leisure.

- ✦ You need the money.
- ✦ You miss having the routine of a job.
- ✦ You miss the daily human contact.
- ✦ Your days seem empty.
- ✦ You miss the meaning and direction a job seemed to offer.

Those are all good reasons. And starting a business or taking on a part- or full-time job may be in order. But before you act, it might be helpful to explore your options a little more deeply.

- *The cost of earning more money*. Although the extra money brought in by a business or a new job might be useful, take into account the *outgoing* expenses involved in your own business or working outside your home. In a business there are multiple expenses—supplies, taxes, phones, advertising, and more if you hire other people to help with your business. In a new job, the expenditures are very different, but might include commuting costs, lunches, clothing, and possibly even accounting costs when you start filing tax returns again. Remember that any additional income might affect your taxes and government benefits, so you should check with a Social Security counselor.

- *The cost of routine*. You may miss the structure of being at a certain place at a certain time to perform certain tasks. Thirty or forty years of obeying the clock is a very strong habit. But that may also have been one of the things you disliked about your job. If you're thinking about returning to a work routine, make sure that you're not stepping back into the frying pan. Consider whether the new routine you want is one that can excite you and meet your needs, not deaden you and eliminate any time you may want for yourself.

- *The cost of human contact*. Missing human contact is one of the most common problems of retirement. It might be a special problem if your job was a highly social one, was in a busy office, or was with people you especially liked and admired. But there may have been days when your coworkers got on your nerves so much that you almost wished for a job on a desert island. Remember that human nature hasn't changed just because you've retired. Don't romanticize the allure of working with others. It may be a payoff, but it also may not be paradise.

Although the extra money brought in by a business or a new job might be useful, take into account the outgoing expenses involved in your own business or working outside your home.

*   *The cost of returning to work.* There's a world of opportunity out there for the retiree. If you've worked through *The Healing Journey Through Retirement* to this point, you've been exposed to and written about some of the other options available to you in your retirement. A return to work in any capacity, even as a part-time worker or a volunteer, implies some level of commitment to your new work environment. This means less time for yourself, less time for your relationships, and less time and energy to pursue other interests.

If you think that you might want to return to work in some way, use the journal entries in this chapter to think about and think through your ideas.

DO YOU WANT TO RETURN TO WORK?

1. Do you want to return to work in some capacity or develop your own business? If not, skip this entry and come back to it if you later decide that you want to think further about returning to work or developing your own business.

_____

_____

_____

2. Why do you want to return to work? Check all that apply.

___ bored without work

___ don't know what else to do

___ emotional security of a paycheck

___ need a regular paycheck to make

    ends meet

___ want the routine

___ want the status of having a job

___ want to be around people

___ want to develop my own business

___ want to feel useful

___ want to try my hand at something new

other: _____   _____

_____   _____

_____   _____

3. How will you decide if a return to work is for you?

_____

_____

_____

4. If you return to work, how much time do you want to spend in your new job?

_____

_____

_____

5. What *most* motivates you to consider returning to work: the money; the intangibles, such as being with people or doing something of interest; or just because the habit of work is so ingrained?

_____

_____

6. Are you more interested in a job or your own business? Either way, why?

_____

_____

_____

_____

7. If money is not the motivating factor, would volunteer work provide the other pay-offs you're looking for? If it is, refer to or complete the "Giving Your Time" journal entry in Chapter 6.

_____

_____

_____

8. Returning to Question 1 of this entry, do you think you want to return to work after you retire? If so, why? If not, why not?

_____

_____

_____

_____

THINGS TO THINK ABOUT

- What does it _feel_ like to be thinking about or planning a return to work? Does it feel good or bad, right or wrong? Can you let your feelings be your guide in making this decision?
- What do your answers to Question 2 tell you about your needs?
- Is returning to work the thing you most want to do with your retirement? Would returning to work mean avoiding dealing with your retirement and making it work? Are you trying hard enough to make your retirement a success _without_ having to return to work?

What Kind of Job Do You Want?

Older workers have more difficulty getting hired. That may be unfair, and this reality may be based on myths about older workers: They're less reliable, more absent due to illness, and slower to pick up new skills. But it's true, nonetheless, that seniors have a tougher time getting hired. However, older workers _do_ get rehired.

With the understanding that it can be difficult for older workers to get a job and return to the workplace, what kind of job do you want? Do you want to enter a whole new field, or do you want to return to your former job field in another capacity? Whether you seek full- or part-time work, a home-based business or an office environment, or whether you'd rather volunteer your time and energy than take home a paycheck, knowing your-self is the key.

Use the next journal entry to develop a simple inventory of your interests, which may help you decide where and how you could best help yourself and others. Try to forget for a moment what you did before retirement and instead answer as if starting over. You're getting a second chance—except now you're a lot wiser than you were in your late teens or twenties.

WHAT KIND OF JOB WOULD BE RIGHT FOR YOU?

1. What kind of work do you prefer? Although the items are grouped into pairs of opposites, the following list is intended only to help you organize your thinking. Check *all* that apply, even if the things you check off seem like contradictions.

___ using my hands

___ analysis and creative thinking

___ working with ideas and concepts

___ working on a team

___ organizing and planning

___ supervision and training

___ less detail and more general work

___ being responsible for my own efforts

___ working with chaos and constant change

other: _____

_____

_____

_____

___ working with my mind

___ following clearly developed plans

___ working with numbers, data, and records

___ working alone

___ taking direction from others

___ taking the lead from others

___ focus on general tasks and not detail

___ being responsible for the efforts of others

___ working in predictable environment

_____

_____

_____

_____

2. What sorts of things about work most interest you?

_____

_____

_____

_____

3. What sorts of jobs or businesses have been your most fulfilling?

_____

_____

_____

4. What jobs or lines of work have you always wanted to try?

_____

_____

_____

_____

5. What job-related skills do you have?

___artistic/design	___fund raising	___public speaking
___bookkeeping	___gardening	___secretarial
___building and repair skills	___grant writing	___selling
___business management	___language/interpretation	___serving food
___coaching sports	___marketing	___sports
___computer skills	___mechanics	___teaching
___cooking	___music	___training
___counseling	___organizational skills	___word processing
___day care	___public relations	___writing

other: _____   _____

_____   _____

_____   _____

6. What special interests, training, or hobbies do you have that you can incorporate into a new job or business?

_____

_____

_____

7. What kind of work can you handle physically? What kind of work can you handle emotionally?

_____

_____

_____

8. Looking back at your answers in this entry, what sort of work or business do you most want to be involved in?

_____

_____

_____

9. How seriously will you pursue returning to work or developing a business?

_____

_____

_____

THINGS TO THINK ABOUT

- Do you have a sense of the kind of work or business you'd like to return to? Are you *ready* to return to a work environment?
- Do you need more training or skill development before doing the kind of work or developing the kind of business you'd most like?
- Are there any special constraints on the kind of work you can do, such as physical problems, medications, dietary needs, prosthetic devices, or the length of time you can work without a break?

A Word about Possibilities

Now that you've had some time to think about whether you want to return to work and your interests and skills, begin to narrow down your choices. Perhaps you can eliminate some possibilities right away. For example, let's say you don't particularly enjoy young people or teaching. That's an avenue you can disregard.

Perhaps you really like pets. You remember that you enjoyed yourself when you did some volunteer work at an animal shelter a while back. And perhaps you're an energetic self-starter who's free to work irregular hours or days and who doesn't necessarily want to get back into the office grind. Maybe you could work at a pet store, start your own pet store or buy an existing one, start a pet-sitting service that comes to pet owners' homes while they're on vacation, or manufacture some product that would help pets and pet owners.

Or, perhaps you *do* like children and teaching. Furthermore, art and travel have been your passions for years. Could you hold art classes for kids in your home? Could you instruct adults at a local community center or community college? Could you organize art tours for artists, or art tours for other art lovers? If writing is among your skills, could you write about local art happenings for a small newspaper or magazine? The possibilities are there if you think about them. Review your last journal entry, try to make connections among your answers, and see what you come up with.

A Word about Finances

One of the major drawbacks to returning to work is that you may lose all or part of your Social Security benefits.

One of the major drawbacks to returning to work is that you may lose all or part of your Social Security benefits. That's because Social Security is an *insurance,* not an annuity. That is, it's designed as a safety net, not a guaranteed payment if you don't really need it. A further reality is that while Social Security benefits are not taxable, money you earn at your job or business is.

The rules about both taxes and Social Security are complicated and riddled with exceptions and special provisions. So remember, before you make any firm decision, you should talk to your local Social Security office as well as your tax accountant or professional financial adviser.

A Word about Families

Whatever you decide about working or not working, discuss it fully with your spouse and family. There's the financial angle, of course, that may affect you all. But with your decision may also come altered expectations. Perhaps your spouse is looking forward to spending more time with you, or maybe your children are hoping you can help with your grandkids. Or, conversely, maybe they're dreading the prospect of having you home twenty-four hours a day without much to do.

In either event, handling two jobs—the one expected of you at home and the one in the labor market—is no easy task. If you decide to return to work in any form, be sure your family understands and, hopefully, approves of your decision and what it means for your family's lifestyle.

Whatever you decide about working or not working, discuss it fully with your spouse and family.

THE PRICE

1. How might your decision to return or *not* return to work affect other people, especially your spouse or other family members?

_____

_____

_____

_____

2. What sorts of difficulties might be raised for you by returning to work?

_____

_____

_____

_____

3. What sorts of difficulties or problems might be raised for your spouse or other family members?

_____

_____

_____

4. In returning to work, what do you gain and what do you lose?

a. *I will gain . . .* _____

_____

_____

b. *I will lose . . .* _____

_____

_____

5. Is it important to return to work or a business? If so, why? If not, why not?

_____

_____

_____

THINGS TO THINK ABOUT

- Do you have support from family or friends in a decision to return to work?
- Is a decision to return to work or start a business worth it? Do the gains outweigh the possible losses?
- Do you have other choices for how to use your time or extend your money so you don't *have* to return to work?

Finding a Job

Let's assume you want to return to a full- or part-time job rather than a business of your own. You'll need to prepare a resume and letters of application, of course. You'll also want to think about what you will say and what points you'll try to make in a job interview. Before you get that far, you have to find jobs that interest you enough to even apply.

You can look in the classifieds, of course. And one of your first stops should be your state employment office; ask if it has an "older worker" specialist. But don't stop there. Try to get help from every possible source, such as the following:

- Friends, relatives, club or lodge members, clergy, or anyone else you can think of. You've got to have a lot of hooks in the water to catch a fish.

- Former employers. Ask them for a letter of recommendation and for any suggestions they might have on either specific leads or general areas you might investigate.

- Reputable private employment agencies. Register with them.

- Executive search firms. If you're qualified for an executive position, contact them. They're in the Yellow Pages, but be aware of the agencies that charge a fee even *before* they find you a job.

- Anyone who's leaving a job. Ask if they'd be comfortable recommending you as a replacement.

- Companies or organizations that have rejected you. They may not have had openings that were right for you, but they might have suggestions for other places to look.

- The chamber of commerce. It probably has a list of appropriate firms in your field.

If you're qualified for an executive position, contact executive search firms. They're in the Yellow Pages, but be aware of the agencies that charge a fee even before they find you a job.

- Local, state, and federal government. Government at all levels is one of the largest and most impartial employers of older workers. So check out whether there's a job hotline or job coordinator at your city, county, and federal offices.

Part-Time Possibilities

Working part-time brings many advantages. For one thing, a part-time job can bridge the gap between being fully retired, earning additional money, or productively using your time and staying busy. Part-time work can provide a middle ground if you're interested in both working *and* having time for yourself. It can also serve as a testing ground that can help you decide if you want to go back into the full-time workforce, experiment with a new field or interest, or learn new job skills.

Many such part-time jobs exist in the service industry. These jobs, in places like churches, schools, hotels, restaurants, and libraries, generally pay less than work in other fields, but the needs of a retiree who doesn't want to give up all his or her leisure time often coincides with those of small businesses or nonprofit organizations who can't afford or don't need full-time help. If you can be flexible in your working hours, you might have a leg up. Evening work, for example, is often scorned by young people.

Remember seasonal work, too. Try post offices during the holidays, tax-preparation firms in March and April, department stores before Christmas, and camps and resorts in the summer. Census takers are in demand every four years, and polling places want workers at election time.

You can also register with temporary-help services. They find temporary assignments for you at a variety of firms. Having typing, bookkeeping, or other business skills makes you especially valuable. And it's not unusual for a temporary stint to lead to a

Part-time work can provide a middle ground if you're interested in both working and having time for yourself.

permanent assignment, if that's your desire. In addition, some types of part-time jobs are especially accessible to the retired worker. Selling, for example, by its nature attracts independent people who like to set their own hours. Real estate is especially flexible, provided you can work on weekends and sometimes at night, and licensing is generally required.

Increasing the Chances for Success

A retired worker has the best chance of making money doing something he or she already knows. If you can no longer handle the work in your previous occupation, or if opportunities no longer exist there, you maybe able to use your knowledge in a new way. For example, a teacher might sell textbooks or school equipment, a trucker might become a freight dispatcher, a former salesman might consult as a sales trainer and motivator, or an engineer might become a computer technician who makes house and office calls. Alternatively, consider using your personal interests as the basis for finding a job. For instance, consider working in a bookstore if you're a serious reader, or a hardware store if you're a dedicated putterer. Examine your skills and interests and think about how they might be transformed into a productive, successful, and satisfying return to the work world.

Examine your skills and interests and think about how they might be transformed into a productive, successful, and satisfying return to the work world.

On the other hand, you may decide, before or after you start your job hunt, that you need more schooling. If you find you're being turned down for work due to a lack of specific skills, consider more education or training. Maybe just a refresher course will do, or perhaps you need complete retraining for a new occupation. Increasingly, college is for everyone. Junior and community colleges in particular offer many vocational and adult education courses.

Starting Your Own Business

The lure of running one's own business is especially strong for retirees with some capital to invest and a desire to be their own boss. The federal Small Business Administration (SBA) is a *must* resource for anyone considering this route. The SBA lists ten characteristics for the would-be businessperson:

- a positive and pleasant attitude
- leadership skills
- organizing ability
- industry
- responsibility
- good decision-making capability
- sincerity
- perseverance
- physical energy

An eleventh helpful trait might be luck. Most small businesses fail, often due to lack of capital and/or inept marketing. The operation of a business is no easy task. You'll need knowledge, experience, and managerial skills. You'll need to know how to read and understand financial statements and be familiar with cash flow and how to budget expenses and income. If you want to start a new business, you will want to take a look at your own assets —financial, educational, and psychological. If you notice areas in which you're particularly weak, you may want to consider taking on a partner.

If you want to start a new business, you will want to take a look at your own assets— financial, educational, and psychological.

You should also take a look at which fields are growing, such as health, nutrition, workforce training, and technology. But, in the survival-of-the-fittest world of the marketplace, businesses can become so trendy and numerous that the less efficient, less well-managed, less savvy, and less well-funded ones quickly disappear. For instance, think about how many coffeehouses, video rental stores, and yogurt parlors have come and gone in your town. You want to be ahead or atop the crest of the wave, not behind it.

Operating Your Own Business

There are many risks in starting or buying your own business. In fact, there are lots of reasons *not* to start your own business. But, for the right person, the advantages can outweigh the risks.

- You're the boss.
- Your hard work and long hours directly benefit you rather than increasing profits for someone else.
- The earnings potential is less limited.
- There are challenges and endless variety making life both exciting and scary.

If you're at all interested in setting up your own business, your next stop should be the SBA. The intricacies of starting and running your own business are way beyond the scope of this book, but the SBA produces many excellent pamphlets and programs about all kinds of businesses and business procedures. If you qualify, also ask for information about special programs for women or minorities.

What the SBA will emphasize is *really* learning all aspects of a business before you jump in. You'll want to get as well-rounded a picture as possible of what your chances and your challenges will be. So, if you're fascinated about a kind of business but know little about it, you might want to work for a while with somebody who's already doing it. At the very least, you should spend a lot of time talking with businesspeople in the same or related fields, as well as with banks and with your potential customers.

If you're fascinated about a kind of business but know little about it, you might want to work for a while with somebody who's already doing it.

Another way to get into business is to buy one that's already operating. If the owner is selling for reasons unrelated to business prosperity, you could luck out. You can find businesses to buy in the classifieds, through business brokers (listed in the Yellow Pages), through wholesalers who supply businesses, and through trade associations. But make sure you're not taking over a sinking ship. Before you even consider a deal, you should have every aspect of the business studied by an attorney, an accountant, or others who can give you a solid evaluation.

Yet another route is franchising, which has grown tremendously in popularity. These businesses remove some of the risk because you're dealing with a known name and getting some help from the franchisor. But the same sort of due diligence is required in franchises as with any other business. Although previous experience is probably less important in a franchise than in a brand new business, energy is in great demand. Be prepared to work long hours, six or seven days a week.

Many people set up mail-order businesses, and more and more Internet businesses are springing up. Regardless of what kind of business or how you start or set it up, the SBA can offer you loads of material and opportunities to learn.

DO I WANT MY OWN BUSINESS?

1. What advantages are there to your starting or buying your own business?

_____

_____

_____

_____

_____

2. What product, service, or field most interests you as a business venture?

_____

_____

_____

_____

3. How much time, effort, and energy do you want to put into a business?

_____

_____

_____

_____

4. Is your family aware that starting a business may cause strains on your time, your availability, your health, and/or on your household's finances?

_____

_____

_____

_____

5. Is starting or buying your own business a serious option now or in the future?

_____

_____

_____

_____

6. What are the greatest limitations or obstacles to owning a business?

_____

_____

_____

_____

_____

7. What do you need to do to further pursue the idea of a business?

_____

_____

_____

_____

_____

_____

_____

8. How do you *feel* about the idea of business? Does it seem realistic, exciting, overwhelming, a great idea for the future, too difficult, just right, something to think about?

_____

_____

_____

_____

_____

_____

_____

_____

THINGS TO THINK ABOUT

- If you're still thinking about a business, what kind? Direct, mail-order, or Internet, home-based or commercial building? Do you know enough about the type of business you want to own?
- Do you have the support you'll need to start a business: financial and emotional? Are your family and friends supportive?
- What might you be risking by starting or buying a business? Can you *afford* to take this risk?

Volunteering Your Time

As not every retiree returns to work for the income, volunteer work is an excellent way to use your time in an unpaid job that can be both personally rewarding and of immense value to others. Although an earlier generation may not have understood the concept of working for nothing, that's a narrow view. For one thing, volunteering is a good way to learn about an area of business. Second, volunteering can also lead to a paid job, if that's your goal. And, even if you don't aspire to work for pay or start your own firm, volunteering is a way to try out something new and different, a way to test your skills, your experience, your reliability, your maturity, and way to give to others who may need your help.

If you completed Chapter 6, "Discovering All You Can Do," you've already considered volunteer work. If you do decide to volunteer, you probably will do so with a good deal of hope and idealism. But not every organization uses its volunteers well. You don't want to sign up to find yourself just making coffee for the paid personnel when you thought you were going to be doing something more meaningful. To make your volunteering a pleasant experience, you should scrutinize the commitment with the same critical eye that you'd use to assess a paying job.

Volunteer projects are as numerous and varied as your imagination. One of our nation's best-known volunteers is former president Jimmy Carter, who's helped negotiate an end to political conflict, monitored foreign elections, and built homes for the needy. "Volunteer work takes us out of our self-enclosed protected environment," Carter says. "My biggest reward has come from breaking down the barriers between rich people like me and poor people whom we otherwise never would have met." Remember that there may be a local volunteer bureau, a Retired Senior Volunteer Program (RSVP), or a United Way in your

To make your volunteering a pleasant experience, you should scrutinize the commitment with the same critical eye that you'd use to assess a paying job.

It's crucial that you investigate as thoroughly as possible every lead that interests you. You want to make a good choice and not suffer either a financial or a psychological setback.

community if you're interested in learning more about volunteer opportunities.

Going Forward

By now, you may have an idea of what jobs or businesses or volunteer opportunities attract you. It's crucial that you investigate as thoroughly as possible every lead that interests you. You want to make a good choice and not suffer either a financial or a psychological setback. Whatever you decide, look ahead with patient optimism. As Ethel Percy Andrus, founder of the American Association of Retired Persons, said: "A man cannot go forward and stand still looking backwards at the same time." Like any other organ, the brain responds to use and exercise, and the world of work and volunteerism can give you a chance to keep yours in shape.

CHECKPOINT: TO WORK OR NOT TO WORK

1. Have you figured out whether you can make the money you need working for someone else or working for yourself, or if you even have to work for pay?

_____

_____

_____

2. Can you get your psychological needs fulfilled without returning to work or owning a business? Do you *need* to work?

_____

_____

3. Does your family go along with your plan, whatever it is?

_____

_____

4. How does your decision affect your overall goals for retirement, including the quality and quantity of your time for leisure, family, travel, and personal growth?

_____

_____

_____

_____

_____

5. What do you *most* want, to return to work or remain in full retirement? Are you ready to make a choice?

_____

_____

_____

_____

_____

THINGS TO THINK ABOUT

- Have you spent enough time thinking about a return to work? Have you spent enough time discussing it with family and friends?
- Are you ready to make this sort of decision now? Do you even *have* to make this decision at this time? Is returning to work an idea to come back and visit at a later time?

9

Destination:

REDEFINING YOUR MARRIAGE

"Seldom, or perhaps never, does a marriage develop . . . smoothly and without crises; there is no coming to consciousness without pain."
——CARL JUNG

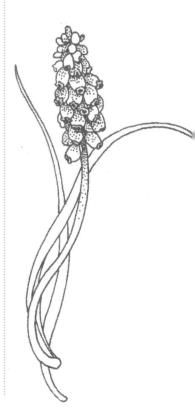

DOUG

I was the vice president of a small chain of art galleries when my wife Bernice retired as the director of a nonprofit group and took a part-time job as a lobbyist. But she found lobbying unsatisfying and thought more and more about moving back down South, where she was raised. As soon as I became eligible for early retirement, she told me that she was quitting work and going to Florida, with or without me, for at least the winters. I knew she meant it, and decided I didn't want to stay in Massachusetts shoveling snow each winter and talking to myself. So I took the early retirement and went to Florida with Bernice. In a perfect world, I would have stayed longer at my company and perhaps become president. But I understood Bernice's needs, and I valued our relationship more than the last few years on my job. Transitioning to retirement turned out to be difficult for me, but faced with the same situation I'd do it again, because Bernice and I have become even closer.

JANICE

Jack's retirement seemed great at first. I have to say, though, that the idea didn't last long. With him home all day, my whole life got turned upside down because his life got turned upside down. He was used to being served expensive business lunches and expected the same from me. Until then, I was used to running the house the way I saw fit and usually made a quick sandwich for lunch. That little difference quickly became an irritant we didn't know how to handle. Worse, that was only one of a whole host of problems for us that we just never expected.

THERE'S A POPULAR belief that retirement is difficult because married couples get on each other's nerves. Like many stereotypes, there's a germ of truth in that myth, but that's as far as it goes. In fact, research has found that only a small proportion of marriages grow worse after retirement. Nevertheless, even strong marriages can begin to show stress when one or both partners retires. Suddenly the couple may occupy the same space twenty-four hours a day, upsetting the delicate balance between dependence and independence. Or the pair may find that their dreams, long held but rarely discussed, are in conflict. At best, there's some serious adjustments to be made; at worst, such disputes can erupt into outright war zones.

"I married for love, but not for lunch," Mrs. Casey Stengel reportedly said after her baseball-manager husband retired. And that sums up the feeling of many spouses, male or female, who feel their independence eroding. In addition, the habits of one spouse, such as excessive talking, dressing sloppily, or fiddling with the remote control, may be tolerable for short periods of time but become unbearable as a steady diet.

In other words, the relationship after retirement changes from two people being together but independent to two people sharing one life together. Couples can, however, find ways to make this total togetherness enriching. While there are pitfalls to the sudden change in household routine, there's potential, too, for greater enjoyment of one another's company. Many couples, in fact, can find a new intimacy.

The relationship after retirement changes from two people being together but independent to two people sharing one life together.

Adapting to Change

Most marriages do change after retirement, and discord can follow if the couple isn't able to adjust to new roles. Not surprisingly, how well the partners got along *before* retirement—their tolerance for one another, their mutual respect, their communication, and their commitment—is critical. When major marital conflict does occur *during* retirement, it's likely to be a continuation of long-standing problems that were ignored or unresolved *before* retirement.

The keys to a successful postretirement marriage are honesty, empathy, and an effort to anticipate the changes in the rhythms of your own routine and those of your partner. And it's important to start as early as possible to minimize conflict. Think about the strains that retirement will bring. Think about habits that may require change, but that are difficult to actually change. Think about the importance of each partner's ability to accommodate each other for the sake of the relationship and how to successfully address matters large and small in their relationship.

It's critical to learn to resolve large issues that affect both partners in a committed relationship, but it's just as important to deal with the small things that make up the texture and quality of everyday life. Some spouses need to learn, for example, not to nag, but to instead *negotiate* on small issues such as when lunch will be prepared and by whom. Large matters must be discussed and resolved in the same way, with negotiation and communication as the keys, not nagging, coercion, or domination. The resolution of critical issues such as where you will live, how you will spend your vacations, and who chooses what you can or can't afford are matters that require tact, sensitivity, openness, and sometimes negotiation.

Both partners need to learn to talk openly and frankly about issues that are potentially sensitive. For instance, what is the

How well the partners got along before retirement—their tolerance for one another, their mutual respect, their communication, and their commitment—is critical.

emotional impact on the retired spouse if the other continues to work, especially if it's the wife who continues to work in a marriage where the husband was the traditional breadwinner? In a relationship where roles have been strictly defined along traditional gender lines, is each partner secure enough in his or her gender role to share kitchen duties or not object when the husband's friends come over to watch sports or the wife's bridge club meets in the home? And sensitive issues go far beyond these, including intimacy in your relationship and the importance and role of sex in your lives together. These are potentially powerful issues in *any* relationship. In all this, your ability to communicate your needs and express your ideas, listen to one another, and manage inevitable conflict are all critical areas in this new era in your marriage. Now it's going to be especially important to be flexible and open to growth.

Understanding Your Relationship

Before you can really understand other people, you have to understand yourself. The same is true for your relationship. To reach out and improve your relationship, you first have to understand it. This is a complex task at any stage in life, and it would be a mistake to think that *understanding* relationships equals *having* good relationships. If that were so, every psychologist would have winning relationships that never failed. Nevertheless, whether you want to change or develop a relationship, understanding how it works is an important tool that can help.

As you explore your relationship, you'll be more able to identify what you need, what you want, and how you feel. But it's as important to understand the point of view, feelings, and needs of your spouse, because relationships are a two-way street. It's not just how *you* feel or just what *you* want.

Use the next journal entry to begin exploring your relation-

To reach out and improve your relationship, you first have to understand it. However, it would be a mistake to think that understanding *relationships equals* having *good relationships.*

ship, communication skills, and expectations. As you're in a relationship—which is the whole point of this chapter—it will be important to share your feelings and thoughts with your partner if you can. This next entry does require you to share at least some of your thoughts with your spouse in order to meaningfully complete the entry.

TALKING TO ONE ANOTHER

1. Check off the answer that most typically describes your discussions in general and on difficult issues.

	Often	Sometimes	Rarely	Never
Do you talk about issues in the relationship?	___	___	___	___
Do you feel you can speak honestly?	___	___	___	___
Do you avoid harsh words and accusations?	___	___	___	___
Do both parties get an equal chance to share?	___	___	___	___
Do you feel your partner really listens to you?	___	___	___	___
Do *you* really listen to your partner?	___	___	___	___
Do you disagree on matters?	___	___	___	___
Do you feel good about one another after you talk?	___	___	___	___
Do your discussions wind up on a good note?	___	___	___	___
Do your disagreements end with resolution?	___	___	___	___
Do you compromise more than you want to?	___	___	___	___
Does you spouse compromise more than you?	___	___	___	___
Do your talks end in an action plan?	___	___	___	___
Are there leftover problems after you talk?	___	___	___	___
other: _____	___	___	___	___
_____	___	___	___	___
_____	___	___	___	___

2. What pattern can you see from your answers? What do your answers tell you about your relationship and how well you communicate with each other?

_____

_____

_____

_____

_____

3. Do you feel that either you or your partner need to improve your communication skills? If so, in what areas?

_____

_____

_____

_____

_____

4. You and your partner may see your respective roles differently, and your roles may change with retirement. The more you know about what you want from your partner and what your partner wants from you, the better you can adjust. Check off the answer that most typically describes *your* expectations of yourself or your partner with respect to the roles you each play in your relationship.

	I should	My partner should	We both should
be a friend and confidant	___	___	___
be more independent of each other	___	___	___
bring home a paycheck	___	___	___
do the gift buying	___	___	___
handle our money	___	___	___
keep the house clean	___	___	___
keep the house in good repair	___	___	___

	I should	My partner should	We both should
keep up correspondence with friends/family	___	___	___
maintain our social life	___	___	___
make major family decisions	___	___	___
organize our leisure time	___	___	___
plan more things for us to do together	___	___	___
prepare meals	___	___	___
take care of the yard or garden	___	___	___
other: _____	___	___	___
_____	___	___	___
_____	___	___	___
_____	___	___	___

5. Now discuss your answers with your partner. What are his or her thoughts on the roles you each should play in your relationship?

_____

_____

_____

_____

_____

6. Describe communication within your relationship.

_____

_____

_____

_____

_____

_____

7. Are you satisfied with the level of communication within your relationship and *how* you communicate?

_____

_____

_____

_____

_____

THINGS TO THINK ABOUT

- Do you have free and open communication in your relationship? Can you each be honest without fear of hurting each other's feelings?
- When you compromise, do you both show a willingness to give up something to achieve your aims, or does one partner usually give in just to ensure peace?
- Do you want to adjust your relationship in order to improve it? Do you need help making changes? Could you benefit from seeing a couples counselor or by attending a course on improving communication within your marriage?

The Role of Marriage

Marriage, for some people, is the central feature in their lives. For others, marriage is important but not the defining point around which all else revolves. In other cases, marriage is almost secondary. Of course, the same is true for retirees. Since you're reading this chapter, the chances are good that your marriage *is* important and you want to better understand and/or improve it, especially with the changes introduced by retirement. Use the next entry to help consider what role your marriage plays in your retired life and what role you want it to play.

LOCATING YOUR MARRIAGE

1. *When my partner is away, I most miss . . .* _____

_____

2. *When my partner is away, I most enjoy . . .* _____

_____

3. *The most satisfying parts of our relationship are . . .* _____

_____

_____

4. *The least satisfying parts of our relationship are . . .* _____

_____

_____

5. How are these parts, both satisfying and unsatisfying, being affected by retirement?

_____

_____

_____

_____

6. What retirement activities do you picture . . .

a. doing without your partner? _____

_____

_____

b. doing with your partner? _____

_____

_____

c. your partner doing without you? _____

_____

_____

7. *In my relationship, I want . . .*

a. *more of . . .* _____

_____

b. *less of . . .* _____

_____

8a. Do you see your partner being the central part of your retirement? _____

_____

_____

b. Do you see sacrificing for your partner? _____

_____

c. Do you see being a team where the *us* is more important than the *me*? _____

_____

_____

d. Do you see weathering together whatever storms you encounter? _____

_____

9. Are you satisfied with the role and place of your marriage in your retired life?

_____

_____

_____

_____

THINGS TO THINK ABOUT

- Are you optimistic or concerned about how retirement will affect your relationship?
- Is your vision of retirement compatible with your partner's vision? If it's not, is this something you can talk about?
- Are you comfortable discussing with your partner the pros and cons of the relationship? Would you be more comfortable using a third party, such as a counselor?

Shifts in Family Life

One of a family's most important functions is to provide emotional support to its members. During the working years this means many things, including providing a haven from the stresses of work. During retirement, partners ideally provide companionship to one another and help ease difficulties during this transition.

But retirement itself may create new problems for married retirees and their spouses. Keep in mind that for many retirees marriages have already been in existence for one, two, or three decades. During this time, patterns have developed about who directs the finances, who plans the couple's social life, and who takes care of household duties, among other things. Retirement often disrupts those familiar roles. In fact, just getting used to being together all day creates problems for some. Couples without common interests find the added time together puts more strain on the marriage than when one or both were employed.

Spending so much time together in retirement also underscores the issue of privacy. For instance, the wife who was alone while her husband was working had the freedom to set her own social schedule and to do household tasks according to *her* cadence. With her husband retired, she may no longer have that freedom or independence. She may find herself having to answer questions about what she's doing, where she's going, and when she'll be back, and she may begin to experience this new aspect of her relationship as invasive and galling. And, once retired, husbands tend to participate more in household tasks. For some couples, this is a new and enjoyable common activity; others come to experience it as an irritating change.

Patterns have developed about who directs the finances, who plans the couple's social life, and who takes care of household duties, among other things. Retirement often disrupts those familiar roles.

Turf

Each of the partners needs to find ways to relinquish some of their turf because, for a while at least, they both share the same turf.

In some marriages, there are deeply held values about the proper sphere for each gender; that is, the husband should be the provider and engage in outside chores, while the wife should take care of the children and the home. Such husbands may resent being drawn into what many of them consider women's work. Likewise, wives may not welcome their husbands' encroachment on what they consider their turf. But even in marriages where issues *aren't* strictly based on gender, there's always other patterns of roles and responsibilities that partners have accepted and fallen into over the years. Retirement often brings significant changes to these routines and roles, and the boundaries that marked the turf of each partner begin to blur.

Accordingly, in the early stages of retirement, it's especially important to recognize and respect turf issues, or more correctly the issues that result from *loss* of turf. Each of the partners needs to find ways to relinquish some of their turf because, for a while at least, they both share the *same* turf. The increased amount of time retirees spend with their partners and that shared turf can be a blessing or a curse. The result can be conflict or a greater closeness.

Coping with Change

Once retired, you leave an environment that was externally controlled. Without the rigors and routines of work, you must direct yourself, filling your days with meaningful activities as well as filling the social vacuum created by the loss of work colleagues and relationships. The same is true for both partners in marriages where both have held full-time jobs and both have to adjust to a life free of paid work.

In marriages where only the husband has worked, the situation is a little different. In this common scenario, the wife, usually free by now of the responsibility of raising children, may have developed other interests of her own: a new career, hobby, or more social contact with other people. But with the husband at home all day, she faces a decision about how to spend her time. How does she balance these enjoyable new activities with the time her husband expects her to be with him?

Either way, the couple no longer has work or the children as a diversion. They're really stuck with each other, and they begin to view each other up close, perhaps seeing blemishes and faults they hadn't known before. In addition to the full-time *physical* presence, there's also the full-time *emotional* presence. The moods and strains of one partner may affect the other in a way that feels both oppressive and inescapable. Under such conditions, the potential for conflict is high. While some couples may prefer to suffer in silence, those who manage most gracefully make an effort to learn new communication skills.

Suffering in silence, though, may be an ingrained habit. If so, it's unfortunate because spouses need to not only lessen and deal with the inevitable conflicts, they also need to make some big choices. Retirement is a time for major decision making: finances, traveling, use of leisure time, and perhaps moving; all of these issues cry out for collaboration, not confrontation or sullen silence. Retirement makes important demands for accommodation, negotiation, and compromise. And, in turn, those require expressing feelings honestly as well as showing empathy and support. It's important to talk *with,* rather than *at,* each other.

Retirement makes important demands for accommodation, negotiation, and compromise.

Dealing with the Issues

Retirement also exposes the level of problem-solving skills in the relationship. Creating a new lifestyle brings with it pleasures and pressures. Natural and inevitable tensions will exist, within and outside of the relationship. Old, unresolved issues and feelings may erupt. Outside relationships may evoke jealousy. Hobbies and pursuits that replace time together may be threatening. Financial and legal issues, such as wills, trusts, and in whose name property is held, can also create stress.

Both partners need to be able to see their partner's needs as well as their own. It's likely there will be conflicts along the way, and a willingness and an ability to work through these issues is of prime importance. Remember, partners have a choice: They may take an adversarial, collaborative, or even a head-in-the-sand stance. In fact, some couples survive problems without *ever* addressing or resolving them. Instead, issues are hidden and suppressed under a conspiracy of silence. Others develop a mode of merely *tolerating* problems. Differences are addressed but never actually resolved. They are acknowledged but there are no solutions. Partners simply tolerate problems as they tolerate each other. But, some couples actually *solve* problems by addressing and settling them. These partners discuss issues openly and bring problem-solving skills to bear.

The ability to share your perspective with someone else and hear their point of view offers the opportunity to both experience empathy, or oneness, with that person and the enrichment of your life.

Managing Conflict

The ability to share *your* perspective with someone else and hear *their* point of view offers the opportunity to both experience empathy, or oneness, with that person and the enrichment of your life. In a marriage, these are especially desirable qualities. And where more than one point of view exists, there is the prospect —and even the likelihood—of conflict and clashes.

Conflicts exist and probably always will. They're a fundamental part of any relationship, and although a worthy ideal may be to eliminate conflict entirely, this is almost certainly an unrealistic task. A more realistic goal is to learn how to handle confrontation and resolve conflict so that you can move toward a more harmonious relationship in which conflicts are reduced and easily managed when they do come up. The trick is not to eliminate the conflict, but manage and resolve it.

Often, even when a conflict is dealt with, it just seems to return time and time again. Or new conflicts spring up like brush fires all around you. When seen one way, the goal of conflict management is to ensure that disagreements and fights *don't* get out of hand and *do* get resolved without leaving bad feelings. In a broader sense, though, conflict management involves *learning* about and *understanding* the roots of conflict so that successfully learning to deal with one fight helps you to deal with other conflicts as well. There are four basic steps to conflict management. The fifth step is really about preparing for the *next* conflict.

The goal of conflict management is to ensure that disagreements and fights don't *get out of hand and* do *get resolved without leaving bad feelings.*

- ◆ Conflict recognition. In order to resolve conflict you first have to recognize you're in a conflict, or heading toward one. This is usually the easy part, although not always. Sometimes conflicts are hidden or come out in different ways, and the underlying and sometimes *real* issue remains simmering under the surface unrecognized.

- ◆ Conflict management. Once recognized, you have to be able to *manage* conflict so it doesn't explode into an angry fight that can tear a relationship apart, push the relationship in the wrong direction, *or* go back underground where it once again begins to simmer and brew until its next eruption.

- ◆ Conflict understanding. Many conflicts seem to drag on and on, even though individual skirmishes get settled. The third step along the path to resolution is *understanding* the roots and nature of the conflict so that your attempts at resolution are aimed at the *right* problem. This step requires that you understand the *root* causes of the conflict.

- Conflict resolution. Conflict resolution means addressing and settling the *root* causes of the problem and requires the ability to see things from more than one angle: in this case from your partner's view as well as your own.

- Feedback. Simply put, this is the communication that happens *after* the issue is resolved and the individual conflict settled. This is the calm discussion that can help you to figure out what went wrong, how you both felt, and how to best deal with issues that still need to be resolved *before* the next conflict.

Are you easily able to resolve conflicts or do you need to work more on your conflict resolution skills? Are your conflicts a series of individual, unrelated skirmishes, or are they connected to each other over time, through issues and problems that never seem to get *really* resolved? The next entry will help you to think about your conflict management style and skills as well as the underlying causes of conflicts in your relationship. This is an entry you can use repeatedly or even have your spouse use, so make copies before using the blank.

RECOGNIZING AND MANAGING CONFLICT

1. Describe a recent conflict.

_____

_____

_____

_____

_____

_____

2. Name three indicators that let you know the conflict was on the way *before* it happened:

a. _____

b. _____

c. _____

3. How well did this conflict get managed? Did it become ugly in some way, leave bad feelings, or did you manage to handle it smoothly?

_____

_____

_____

_____

4. How well do you and your partner *usually* handle conflict?

_____

_____

_____

_____

5. Many conflicts seem to drag on and on because there's a prior history. Regardless of the *immediate* cause of this conflict, what *prior* issues led to this conflict?

_____

_____

_____

_____

6. Name three causes that typically underlie your conflicts.

a. _____

b. _____

c. _____

7. Conflict resolution means addressing and settling the *roots* of the issues, requiring the ability to see things from more than one angle. To resolve future conflict:

a. What does your partner need from you?

_____

_____

_____

b. What do you need from your partner?

_____

_____

_____

8. How will you handle your next conflict?

_____

_____

_____

9. List five things you can do to ensure that the root causes of conflicts don't simply go back underground until they next erupt.

a. _____

b. _____

c. _____

d. _____

e. _____

THINGS TO THINK ABOUT

- Have you learned anything from this entry that can help you to more effectively manage and resolve conflict in your relationship?
- Have you discussed the issues that lead to conflict with your partner? Do you ever use feedback as a way to understand the issues that lead to conflict?
- Do you need outside help to develop more effective conflict resolution skills?

Communicate, Communicate, Communicate

If you're not in the habit of being open with your spouse, you've got a lot of work to do to improve communication in retirement. Even if you already communicate, you may need to take that to a higher level now that you'll be together so much. Here are some suggestions that can help improve communication in any relationship, which can lead to a sense of support and togetherness.

- Put a premium on openness. Find ways to be honest, express your feelings, and share your ideas. This can be risky sometimes, but growth often means stretching yourself and taking paths you may never have taken before.

- Share your problems. Perhaps you didn't like to share your day when you worked because you thought your spouse wasn't interested or perhaps you didn't enjoy replaying conflicts from work. But there's seldom been a period when each of you needs more understanding, support, and sensitivity than now.

- Share your daily lives. Share those things in your life that are mildly interesting, funny, sad, or affect you in some way. Share your ideas and explain your feelings about taking out the trash, missing your office colleagues, not working, politics, the football game—*anything*.

- Ask what you can do for each other. Maybe it's something as seemingly inconsequential (to you) as a hug or help with a chore, or maybe it's something bigger, like taking a trip together. Tell your spouse what you need, and ask and encourage your spouse to do the same with you.

- Set aside a time for grievances. Especially if you're a couple who has kept conflict under wraps, set aside a certain time to talk. Then adhere to that schedule to just discuss how you're doing together. Take turns going first. It's important

Ask what you can do for each other. Tell your spouse what you need, and ask and encourage your spouse to do the same with you.

that each person be able to say what he or she thinks before the other disputes or interrupts. It's also important to acknowledge and validate the other person's feelings, even if you don't agree.

- Avoid verbally bruising each other. We're often cruel, even unintentionally, with those with we love. Refrain from insults, put-downs, and expressions of disgust, and avoid generalizations (about men or women, for instance), which are not only stereotypes, but often hurt.

- Boost self-esteem, don't crush it. When it comes to relationship building, naming someone's deficiencies or failures is rarely as effective as praise. Focus on each other's *positive* traits. Find something good to say, catch each other doing something right, and help build self-confidence and boost self-esteem.

- Avoid controlling. Whenever one spouse seeks to always be right, always be the agenda setter, and always be the virtuous one, he or she may feel like a winner—but it's the marriage that loses.

Whenever one spouse seeks to always be right, always be the agenda setter, and always be the virtuous one, he or she may feel like a winner— but it's the marriage that loses.

A New Intimacy

Intimacy requires the sharing of private space and the extension of personal and emotional boundaries to include each other. Like so much else in close relationships, it can be a source of great satisfaction or conflict. However it's experienced in different relationships, in *healthy* relationships intimacy is always a source of great nourishment.

There's no standard for intimacy, no flag that tells you what intimacy is or what it should be. Indeed, although it's a basic ingredient in any meaningful relationship, defining intimacy is not that easy because its meaning varies from relationship to relationship and within relationships over time. In some relationships, intimacy entwined with sex and feelings of closeness may be connected or confused with sexual feelings. In other relationships, intimacy has more to do with shared moments than sexual interactions. In any case, intimacy is linked with feelings of closeness between partners in a relationship. Use the next journal entry to explore and define intimacy in your relationship.

INTIMATE RELATIONSHIPS

1. What does intimacy mean to you?

_____

_____

_____

_____

_____

2. What five behaviors, things, or interactions do you most identify with intimacy?

a. _____

b. _____

c. _____

d. _____

e. _____

3. In a romantic relationship, what is the difference between intimacy and sex?

_____

_____

_____

_____

_____

4. Describe intimacy in your relationship. *In our relationship, intimacy is . . .*

_____

_____

_____

_____

5. In what ways has intimacy in your relationship changed over time?

_____

_____

_____

_____

6. Are you satisfied with the level of intimacy in your relationship?

_____

_____

_____

THINGS TO THINK ABOUT

- Are you nourished by intimacy in your relationship or starved by lack of intimacy?
- Have you talked to your partner about intimacy? What does intimacy means to him or her? If you haven't discussed intimacy with your partner, why not?

Keeping Intimacy Alive

If a marriage is to remain healthy, intimacy cannot become a thing of the past. Intimacy implies a continual commitment, renewal, and constant search for freshness in the relationship. Intimacy is as up to the moment as the relationship itself.

Whatever the degree of intimacy you enjoy, be aware that having an intimate relationship can evoke many fears. There is a fear of being hurt if you open up to someone else, a fear of becoming dependent on someone else, and a fear of rejection. There's also a fear of not knowing how to introduce or reintroduce intimacy into the relationship and a fear of not being able to perform well enough in an intimate relationship. So, if you haven't had a really intimate relationship until now, move in that direction, but move slowly.

What did you learn about intimacy from your last journal entry? Is your relationship fresh? Are you satisfied by the level of intimacy in your relationship? What can you and your spouse do to keep intimacy alive and fresh?

There is a fear of being hurt if you open up to someone else, a fear of becoming dependent on someone else, and a fear of rejection.

STAYING ALIVE

1. How important is intimacy in your relationship?

_____

_____

_____

2. How important is intimacy to your partner?

_____

_____

_____

3. List five things that represent intimacy for your partner.

a. _____

b. _____

c. _____

d. _____

e. _____

4. Name five activities that can keep or reintroduce intimacy in your relationship.

a. _____

b. _____

c. _____

d. _____

e. _____

5. In what ways has the nature of intimacy changed in your relationship since one or both of you retired?

_____

_____

_____

_____

6. What have you discovered about intimacy in your relationship?

_____

_____

_____

_____

7. How can you enrich the intimacy you experience in your relationship?

_____

_____

_____

_____

8. How can your partner deepen your mutual sense of intimacy?

_____

_____

_____

_____

9. What can you now do *together* to sustain and build on your feelings of intimacy?

_____

_____

_____

_____

_____

Sexuality

Over the life of a marriage, sex takes many different forms at different stages and may be shaped by many forces. The role of sex in a relationship may be influenced by the age of the partners, previous sexual experiences, religious beliefs, individual attitudes, health concerns, personal expectations, and other influences in the lives of the partners. But, in couples, a sexual life is always assumed to exist at some point in the relationship. There's no reason to think that sex ends at retirement or before. In fact, for some it begins to flourish again upon retirement.

Use the final journal entry in this chapter to think about the role and nature of your sex life. An entry like this is particularly personal, but remember that this is your journal and for your eyes only unless you choose to share it with someone else. Try to answer each question as openly and honestly as possible.

SEX AND THE RETIRED COUPLE

1. Is sex important in your life at this time?

_____

_____

_____

2. How important is sexual contact in your relationship?

_____

_____

_____

3. How important is sexual contact to your partner?

_____

_____

_____

4. Are you satisfied with your sex life?

_____

_____

_____

5. Is your partner satisfied with your sex life?

_____

_____

_____

6. Is sex something you want to inject into or improve upon in your marriage?

_____

_____

_____

_____

7. Do you ever discuss sex with your partner? If so, are you in agreement about the role or importance of sex in your relationship? If not, why not?

_____

_____

_____

8. Do you think you and your partner should work on improving your sexual relationship? If so, how might you do this?

_____

_____

_____

_____

_____

_____

THINGS TO THINK ABOUT

- Where does sex fit into your relationship? If sex is important, what *kind* of sex?
- Is sex only one part of intimacy in your relationship, the whole thing, or completely unimportant?
- Do you and your partner share the same feelings about sex?
- Do sexual needs or issues create problems in your relationship? If so, how can you best resolve these?

Checkpoint: Retirement in Marriages

Retirement can be seen as the end of a productive life or the start of a new adventure. It can also change the prism through which we see our mates. There's an old saying among soldiers that combat makes good men better and bad men worse. The same might be said of couples in retirement. A bad marriage probably isn't going to get better because the couple has more time together, but a good marriage *might*. Couples who've built a strong relationship, who've worked at their communication skills, and who genuinely view themselves as a team and not as competitors have the best chance of making retirement the best years of their lives.

Marriage is really a *series* of marriages. Just as the early years of marriage differ from the child-rearing years, so, too, will the retirement era be unlike that the career-building years which preceded it. Couples will need to continue to invent their own rules and adjust their roles as they go along. A good marriage is always being reshaped to satisfy the couple's changing needs and wishes.

Dealing with and growing a relationship are difficult but wonderful tasks. Although some relationships just grow naturally, needing no special insights or plans, most are like gardens. They need attention, tending, care, and work. If you found the entries and the idea in this chapter useful and important and want more, consider using *The Healing Journey for Couples*. That book will help you develop a journal shared and developed *with* your partner and can help you focus and pay attention to many aspects and details of your shared relationship.

Couples who've built a strong relationship, who've worked at their communication skills, and who genuinely view themselves as a team and not as competitors have the best chance of making retirement the best years of their lives.

10

Destination:

BEING SINGLE
IN RETIREMENT

CHARLES

When I was in business, I was pretty driven. I was also pretty out-going. After I retired, I found that I really missed those business lunches, which were more about companionship and pleasure than commerce. So I decided to organize weekly get-togethers with some other guys, all about my own age and most retired. We'd share a few beers and talk about politics, sports, and cars. After about a year of these regular gatherings, I realized that I didn't have one really close friend in the whole bunch, someone I could talk to honestly without embarrassment. Despite our camaraderie, which now seemed superficial, we were all quite guarded about our personal feelings. I never married, but I'd been around enough women to know they're much more open and seem to tell each other everything. *I've since concluded that men aren't built that way. We've been brought up to be competitive and self-sufficient. Right now, I think we suffer as a result. Perhaps the result for me is having many companions but few friends.*

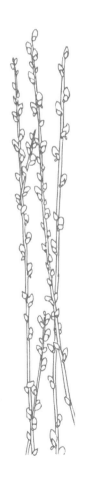

AMY

I was a strong and successful person when I worked in what I saw as a man's world. I headed a division at a pharmaceutical giant and was very active in my professional organization. I was proud of the number of employees I managed, my salary and the other perks I earned, and the sensitivity about women's issues I'd brought to the firm. I was seen and treated as a role model for younger women in the organization. The flip side to these triumphs was that I moved frequently as job opportunities and promotions came and put down few roots. I felt wedded to my job and never married, and most of my friends were coworkers. When retirement came, I had the money and time to enjoy myself. But, I lacked the ability to relax and someone to relax with. I have no relationships, so to speak. My whole life had been with the company. Once that was gone, I looked around and couldn't find much to see.

In most societies and for most individuals, isolation and solitude is an unusual state that runs counter to the need to share, learn, and grow through contact with others.

BEING SINGLE BOTH simplifies and complicates the problems of retirement. It simplifies them because you have only yourself to look after. You needn't worry about your in-laws, the health of your spouse, or whether the two of you will get along when you're both home all of the time. You can do what *you* want to do.

On the other hand, you don't have a partner to share things with or lean on, emotionally or financially. You may lack the intimacy of another important person in your life or even the sheer diversion of someone else's trials and triumphs.

Most people, although perhaps not all, have a need to nurture and be nurtured. Being a single retiree often means being deprived of this comfort and at worst, it can mean isolation and loneliness. In most societies and for most individuals, isolation and solitude is an unusual state that runs counter to the need to share, learn, and grow through contact with others. Some people can tolerate isolation and separation, and others even yearn for it, but for many, being single, especially in later adulthood, makes for a lonely and difficult time.

Singleness for the retiree can come from several sources: being a confirmed loner and never getting married, divorce, or through the death of a spouse. For many retirees, the latter two are the most likely reasons for being alone. Of course, in these cases there's often adult children or other family, but these sort of relationships are simply not the same as what's found in marriage or other forms of romantic partnership. Being alone and coping with being single is a special and important concern for many retirees, whose retirement tasks may be that much more difficult as a result.

Retirement and Singlehood

Not everyone enters retirement as a single person. For some, singlehood follows the death of a spouse or a divorce. For many, retirement comes at a time when both partners are aging and the death of a spouse is not an unusual circumstance. Similarly, changes and difficulties in marriages following the retirement of one or both partners are not uncommon. The very change in relationship often brought about by the retirement itself can contribute to stress in the marriage and lead directly or indirectly to a failed marriage. Either way, retired people often have to contend with *becoming* single at some point after their retirement.

Changes and difficulties in marriages following the retirement of one or both partners are not uncommon.

Obviously, the dynamics are somewhat different for those who were always single, as opposed to becoming single, but the outcomes can often be the same: isolation, loneliness, and disconnection from others.

Different Hurdles for Different Genders

The problems of retiring to a single life are very similar in many respects for both men and women. But some of the problems and issues vary by gender. Women, for example, often have invested more of their time and efforts into building and maintaining friendships and family ties, and this can certainly pay off in retirement, as they can receive emotional and social support from these relationships. Men, traditionally less likely to have built such relationships, may be particularly vulnerable if their spouse divorces them or passes away.

Anna Ford, a British journalist, commented that "the world men inhabit . . . is rather bleak. It is a world full of doubt and confusion, where vulnerability must be hidden, not shared; where competition, not cooperation, is the order of the day; where men sacrifice the possibility of knowing their own children and sharing in their upbringing for the sake of a job they may have chosen by chance, which may not suit them and which in many cases dominates their lives to the exclusion of much else." Presumably, women who have chosen the same career-dominated world and work ethic will bear the same fate. But for women who have invested less of themselves in their work and ensured that their world was broader than work alone, retirement may be far easier, reaping the benefits of relationships formed outside of their career.

On the other hand, where divorced or widowed men may be more independent after retirement, women made single by the same circumstances may feel less sure of themselves. Either way, single men and women who have invested their energies into their careers rather than relationships may face the rockiest transition of all, especially if they have no children and few nonwork contacts.

Most of the journal entries in this chapter are intended for those who are single for whatever reason. But this first entry is designed even for those in current marriages or committed relationships. Whether married or single, the entry will help you to start thinking about your relationships and the possibility of future singlehood.

THE SINGLE LIFE

1. If your spouse or partner were to pass away or seek a divorce, would you be prepared? If this has already happened to you, *were* you prepared?

_____

_____

2. Who could you turn to for help and support if you were suddenly alone in your retirement? Who did you turn to if you have been left single?

_____

_____

_____

_____

3. Do you have the skills to run your household alone? In what areas do you lack knowledge? Were you left high and dry if you entered singlehood after retirement?

_____

_____

_____

_____

4. Do you know what your spouse knows about running the house, taking care of the finances, looking after the kids, caring for the pets? If left single after retirement, did you find yourself helpless, uncertain, or overwhelmed about running the household?

_____

_____

5. Do you/did you have enough close family members, friends, and other relationships to sustain you as a single person?

_____

_____

6. Is it important to develop more friendships and important relationships now?

_____

_____

7. Is loneliness a significant problem for you, or do you expect it to be?

_____

_____

THINGS TO THINK ABOUT

- Do you know the location of the bank accounts, the deeds to the house and other important documents, and who to contact for repairs and service on your home? What else do you need to know about how your household runs?
- What are you doing to plan for support and relationships if you become single? What are you doing to ensure you have relationships and support in your life if already single?
- If depression or substance abuse have entered your life as a result of singlehood, have you considered seeking help from both friends and professionally?

The Single Retired Woman

Retirement has largely been a privilege afforded to men until recently. To become a retired woman, you have to first spend a lifetime being a *working* woman. The retired career woman is a relatively recent phenomenon because *career woman* itself is a relatively new idea. In the traditional middle-class family, the wife either never worked outside of the home or worked only briefly or sporadically. She "retired" with her husband. But that scenario has been turned upside down. Many marriages end in divorce long before either spouse reaches retirement age, and increasing numbers of women have chosen to remain single and never marry.

Given the evolving nature of the full-time working woman, she still faces many obstacles in the workplace. These range from lower pay for equal work, the need to sometimes act as men do in the workplace, the commitment to work that can exclude family relationships, and the very fact that the career woman still stands out, often in stereotyped caricatures. For the retiring woman who has had to work especially hard to overcome these barriers and perhaps work doubly hard to be seen as successful and receive an equal wage, a sudden return to the home can, and often does, affect her self-esteem. She's suddenly inherited the very life she may have sought to escape through work.

For the retiring woman who has had to work especially hard to overcome these barriers and perhaps work doubly hard to be seen as successful and receive an equal wage, a sudden return to the home can, and often does, affect her self-esteem.

Here, perhaps being single is an advantage. No stereotyped housewife roles to fall back into, no dinners to cook for a husband, no selflessly taking care of someone else's needs. But, being a single retired woman can also mean a sudden plunge into life without direction or support. And, because retired women are often financially less well-off than their male counterparts, their chances for travel or moving to a new location may be more limited, reinforcing the idea that now they're trapped in the home. Being single and retired means going it alone.

Through her work, the single woman may have found fulfillment and responsibility and defined an identity beyond that of an unmarried woman. She wasn't judged by society as undistinguished or a failure for not having married or paired up with someone. Having had that self-sufficiency and healthy self-image is certainly a plus in retirement, but losing the identity and distinction provided by work may turn the retired single woman from a success in her career to a woman who never married or had kids.

For the retired single woman, the question arises: Who will take care of her after retirement, and who will she take care of in return? The former career woman may also face the challenge

As a single woman in a couple's world, the single woman is the odd person out. As a single retired person, she may feel very different than her counterparts.

of developing a supportive, understanding, and personally fulfilling support group. When she was working, the career woman was probably with people all day and often took work home. Much of life and support was focused around work. Now she may find that other women her own age are either married or have never experienced life the way she has and have significantly different interests and ways of doing things. As a single woman in a couple's world, the single woman is the odd person out. As a single retired person, she may feel very different than her counterparts.

For the single retired woman, finding a niche or a comfortable role may be especially difficult. The divorced or widowed retired woman may have an easier time in this respect. Both are likely to have a larger family structure than the career woman who never married, and they may have children or even grandchildren. If widowed, the retired woman will most likely still have her husband's family in her life, as well as her own. In this respect, there may be many more already developed *family* relationships and roles to fall back on. Nevertheless, as a retiree, she'll face the same sort of problems as any other retired woman in developing *new* relationships in retirement.

For some women, finding themselves alone is a frightening or an unsatisfying state from which they wish to move. But for other women, being alone is liberating, allowing many possibilities, from no relationship at all to multiple relationships. For still others, singleness allows immersion in friendships and acquaintanceship, and the activities of the larger community may take the place of a single intimate relationship. The beauty of all this is *choice*. Not so long ago (and even now), women were made to feel incomplete, undesirable, or abnormal if they weren't married or didn't have a long-standing romance, especially women who had *never* been married. This prejudice may still exist, but with the changes brought over the past two decades by the women's movement and an increased interest in and understanding of women's psychology and issues, there are many more options of every kind for women today, including midlife sexual relationships. For women of all ages today, the opportunities for relationships, romance, intimacy, and sexuality are more varied than they've ever been before.

The Single Retired Man

The male retiree, whether never married, widowed, or divorced, may have it easier in some respects than his female equivalent. For one thing, he's often more financially secure than women in a similar situation. In addition, he's likely the object of a great deal of matchmaking by friends and acquaintances. And right or wrong, there's also less social stigma attached to being a single male of retirement age; similarly, older men have less trouble attaching to a romantic partner of his own age or younger than older women. Women are eager to connect with him because there's a shortage of men (women who've lost their husbands outnumber widowers five to one), so he gets more dinner invitations and is perhaps less of a social outcast than his female retired peer.

On the other hand, while his evenings may be full, his days may be long. Single females may have their coffee groups, volunteer work, or women's groups that take up their days, but few equivalent daytime outlets exist for men. So males often must work harder or change their perspective in order to find activities to replace the ritual of going to work. When they were younger, many divorced men, missing their children and family life, often compensated by spending more time at the office. Work was comfortable, familiar, and an easy place to hide out. But, in retirement, there's no escaping to the job.

Males often must work harder or change their perspective in order to find activities to replace the ritual of going to work.

Thinking about Relationships

One of the most significant aspects of life is social interaction—personal relationships that connect you to other people. Without relationships it's hard to even think of someone as being a member of a society. When someone who lives alone retires, that person risks the loss of community connection unless he or she has a set of relationships that exists outside and independent of the work environment. Without that established network of friends, an important task for the single retiree is building that network.

Relationships have been a constant theme throughout *The Healing Journey Through Retirement,* and if you've worked your way through the book up until this point, you've already thought and written a great deal about your relationships and their meaning in your life. Use this next entry to generally consider the state of your relationships and whether they meet your needs.

ASSESSING YOUR RELATIONSHIPS

1. Are you satisfied with your current relationships?

_____

_____

_____

2. What do you most want from your relationships? Check all that apply.

__adventure	__intellectual stimulation	__sense of being needed
__comfort	__intimacy	__sense of being valued
__companionship	__love	__sense of importance
__family	__recognition	__sex
__friendship	__respect	__understanding
__fun	__romance	__warmth

other:_____   _____

_____   _____

_____   _____

3. Review what you've just checked off. Summarize your relationship needs.

_____

_____

_____

_____

4. Name your three greatest needs from your relationships.

a. _____

b. _____

c. _____

5. Name your three greatest frustrations with your relationships.

a. _____

b. _____

c. _____

6. What are the most satisfying types of relationships in your life?

_____

_____

_____

_____

7. What are the least satisfying?

_____

_____

_____

_____

8. Now think about each phrase below carefully, and complete each sentence honestly, even if you don't like the answers.

a. *My relationships are . . .* _____

_____

b. *When I think of the sort of relationships I have, I . . .* _____

_____

c. *With my relationships, I most need to work on . . .* _____

_____

d. *If there's one thing I need to change in my relationships, it's . . .* _____

_____

e. *When it comes to my relationships, I need . . .* _____

_____

THINGS TO THINK ABOUT

- Was this an honest appraisal of your relationships? If not, what held you back? If it was, how does your relationship inventory leave you feeling?
- Are you satisfied with your relationships? Is this is an area to work on changing and improving in your new life?
- What have you learned about yourself and your life by reviewing your relationships?

Building or Rebuilding a Network

Having people with whom you share your life and that you can turn to for company, support, and help creates a link with the community around you. This circle of family, friends, acquaintances, and neighbors becomes your network, and in your retirement as a single person it has never before been as important to have a strong network you can interact with and count on. To build, or rebuild, this kind of network, the single, divorced, or widowed retiree *must* learn to become a joiner.

FRIENDS AND ACTIVITIES

1. List ten current relationships in your life. Next to each name, describe the role that person plays in your life, such as friend, family acquaintance, or club member, and then rate the importance of each relationship in your life at this time.

Person	Role	Importance

		Not at All		Somewhat		Very
_____	_____	I	2	3	4	5
_____	_____	I	2	3	4	5
_____	_____	I	2	3	4	5
_____	_____	I	2	3	4	5
_____	_____	I	2	3	4	5
_____	_____	I	2	3	4	5
_____	_____	I	2	3	4	5
_____	_____	I	2	3	4	5
_____	_____	I	2	3	4	5
_____	_____	I	2	3	4	5

2. Are you satisfied with the *types* of relationships you have—that is, friends versus neighbors, family versus acquaintances? Do you wish you had more of a particular type of relationship?

_____

_____

_____

3. Are you satisfied with the *importance* of the relationships you have? Do you have enough important relationships?

_____

_____

_____

4. Do you think you need to work at building some stronger or more well-rounded network of relationships?

_____

_____

5. How can you broaden your network and deepen your friendships?

___attend a support group for retirees   ___spend more time with acquaintances

___attend singles' functions   ___spend more time with current friends

___go to more social gatherings   ___spend more time with family

___join an association or club   ___take a class

___learn more about people in my   ___volunteer my time
    current network

other:_____   _____

_____   _____

6. Are you satisfied by the *quality* of the important relationships in your current life? What can you do to improve the quality of time spent in these relationships?

_____

_____

_____

_____

7. Are there relationships you've neglected that you could restore or improve?

Person	*What You Can Do to Improve This Relationship*
_____	_____
_____	_____
_____	_____
_____	_____
_____	_____
_____	_____

Person	What You Can Do to Improve This Relationship
_____	_____
_____	_____
_____	_____

8. If it's important to contact former friends or colleagues, will this be an awkward or uncomfortable task for you? Why or why not?

_____

_____

_____

_____

9. As you age, it will become increasingly important, and increasingly difficult, to maintain a circle of friends and develop new relationships. In general, how much and what kind of effort do you think you need to put into this work of maintaining a healthy network?

_____

_____

_____

_____

_____

THINGS TO THINK ABOUT

- Are you satisfied with your network? Do you need to work harder to maintain it or build it? Have you considered the future of your network as people in it age and become infirm or pass away?
- What can you do to reach out to other people as you build your future? Will it be awkward or uncomfortable to reach out to existing friends, rekindle old friendships, make new contacts, and get in touch with old acquaintances?
- If you're a parent, are you as close to your kids or grandkids as you'd like to be? If not, what could you do to become closer?

Intimacy in Relationships

Chapter 9, "Redefining Your Marriage," discussed intimacy and sexuality in married relationships. But intimacy isn't restricted to marriages or other committed relationships. Intimacy is a basic ingredient in *any* meaningful relationship, and it comes in every shape and size. Although intimacy is often linked to romance, not every intimate relationship is of a romantic or sexual nature. Parent-child relationships and friendships are examples of intimate relationships that are strictly platonic. In fact, intimacy is linked *more* with feelings of closeness, trust, and shared experiences than romance or sex. However, in long-term romantic relationships, there is usually the assumption that intimacy is, or will be, linked with sexual relations.

Intimacy is linked more with feelings of closeness, trust, and shared experiences than romance or sex.

Intimacy is as available and necessary to single retirees as to those in committed long-term relationships. And, of course, as all retirees age, their long-term relationships will change as spouses, lovers, friends, and family age and pass away. For this reason, the issues surrounding intimacy for the single retiree are no different than those faced by married retirees. If you haven't read Chapter 9, read it now and complete the relevant journal entries that deal with intimacy.

Sexuality in Retirement

With longer life, improved health, changed sexual values, and an increasing focus on sex as the norm, sexual appetite and relations are no longer necessarily *expected* to diminish over time. In other words, sex is as important and as available to the single retiree as it is to anyone else, and often just as necessary. Use the following entry to think about the role of sexuality in your life.

SEX AND THE SINGLE RETIREE

1. What role does sexuality play in your life?

_____

_____

_____

_____

2. Are your sexual needs important to you? Are you satisfied with your sex life?

_____

_____

_____

_____

3. Are sexual relationships available to you? If sex is important to you, in what ways can you get your sexual needs met?

_____

_____

_____

_____

4. How important is it to you to create and maintain an active sex life?

_____

_____

_____

_____

5. How will you cope if sex is important, but currently not available?

_____

_____

_____

_____

6. How will you deal with sexual needs in the future?

_____

_____

_____

_____

THINGS TO THINK ABOUT

- Is there some social pressure to be a sexual person? Do you feel you *have* to have sexual relationships because of social expectations?
- If sex is important, is it important enough to appropriately pursue it? If it's not available, can you live without it?
- Is sex more important than romance? Can you have a romantic relationship without sex?

Joining In

There are real and understandable fears among retirees who are single, divorced, or widowed. These center on how to rebuild and find new relationships outside of work. But being alone doesn't necessarily mean being lonely.

As solitude can be an oppressor, it's imperative for retirees to get out and meet new people. Surviving as a single retiree almost certainly means becoming a joiner. And, while there are many land mines surrounding single, divorced, and widowed retirees, there also are many opportunities. In fact, retirees have more freedom now than they have ever had. They can, depending on their energy and resolve, do almost anything a young single person can: join clubs, return to school, volunteer, date, and remarry. As the population ages and the proportion of seniors grows, we can expect to live in an age in which much of the stigma of being older and single is lifted.

Use the final entry in this chapter to review your status and feelings about being a single retiree and your plans to best deal with this situation.

CHECKPOINT: BEING SINGLE

1. How do you feel about your status as a single retiree?

_____

_____

_____

_____

_____

2. Are you taking care of social needs?	True	False
I'm getting out and meeting new people.	—	—
I'm learning new skills and information.	—	—
I'm largely free of loneliness and/or depression.	—	—
I'm socially active.	—	—
I'm satisfied with how I spend my time.	—	—
I stay in touch with old friends and former colleagues.	—	—
I worry about whether I'll find a partner/spouse.	—	—
I seem to have lost contact with couples, and I miss that contact.	—	—
My self-image is poorer than when I was working.	—	—
I wish I'd kept up contact with old friends, relatives, and coworkers.	—	—
I really need to build a better network of relationships.	—	—
I feel lonely and disconnected.	—	—

3. What have you learned about your relationships?

_____

_____

_____

4. What have you learned about your relationship needs?

_____

_____

_____

5. Do you feel a need to make any substantial changes in your relationships? If so, are you ready to bring about change?

_____

_____

6. How are you feeling as you complete the work in this chapter?

_____

_____

_____

_____

_____

THINGS TO THINK ABOUT

- Is your journaling helping you to focus more on yourself and your needs? Are you getting to know your needs better?
- Are you feeling in control of your life? Are you feeling hopeful or pessimistic? What sort of help, if any, do you need to reach out and connect with people?
- Do you share your thoughts, feelings, and experiences with anyone else? If not, should you be?

11

Destination:

MANAGING FAMILY RELATIONSHIPS

TOM

When Toni, the youngest of our three kids, graduated from college, we thought we'd finally cut the apron strings. But within two years, Toni asked to move back in. Despite going to college, she was in a low-paying job, had no insurance for her run-down car, wasn't saving any money, and lived in a shabby part of town. We had mixed feelings, but we agreed to have Toni live back at home after establishing a set of house rules. The move worked out well for everybody. Toni stuck to the rules, got insurance, started saving for a better car, and began looking for a better paying job. She felt safer in our neighborhood, and instead of paying rent, she began socking away money for a down payment on a small condo. Even though we wanted more privacy in our retirement, we enjoyed Toni's energy and enthusiasm, as well as the fact that she looked after the house when we were away on trips. Plus, when she did move out on her own again, we felt we'd done the right thing.

KEN

About ten years after we retired, my wife Alice became chronically ill and was left physically inactive, as well as withdrawn and de-

203

pressed. One of our five daughters rented a house nearby and moved in with her husband and two children. Much to my delight and my salvation, they came by every day to help out and be part of our lives. Having a willing daughter so close was wonderful.

"THE WORST THING would be to have to depend on my kids," older people sometimes say. Actually, the worst thing is having *no one* to depend on.

Traditionally, the primary caregiver for the retiree has been the spouse. But because people are living longer and divorce is more common, that's no longer a safe assumption. Increasingly, the elderly retiree is looked after by one of his or her children. Or, sometimes it's the retiree who accepts the role of housing and helping the grown children or grandchildren. Equally true, retirees are often responsible for the care of their own elderly parents.

Whatever your family's situation, there are bound to be issues and concerns as one generation accepts responsibility for another. When children live far away, for example, they can't easily provide help even if they want to. What's more, just when the retiree is slowing down, the children, even if close by, are often in the busiest phase of their lives. This may underscore the retiree's already strong feelings about not wanting to become a burden. The children may wish the retiree would spend more time with the grandchildren. But again, physical distance may play a role as does the retiree's need for some privacy and time for self-growth. At the other end of the family spectrum, when retirees take care of their elderly parents, their ability to experience their retirement as they please may be significantly compromised.

Each situation is, of course, unique. But in almost every case, it's wise for the retiree to think about family issues and plan ahead.

Complex Families

Family relationships are more complex than they used to be. With much higher rates of divorce and remarriage, many retirees have stepchildren as well as biological children to think about. That can be a plus or a minus, depending on the personalities involved and the strength of the relationships. For instance, it's not hard to imagine a couple in their late fifties with three college-age children from previous marriages and three more of their own. That's either six people to care *for* or six who could potentially take care *of* the parents.

Within families, many conflicts can occur and resentments linger. The leftovers from earlier days of child rearing may play an active role in the later development of the family and family relationships. For instance, much resentment can be harbored when one child was favored, or *believes* he or she was favored or not favored, over another. Often there's resentment and unease not only between parent and child, but among the siblings as well. Similarly, with the frequency of divorce, there's plenty of room for conflict between stepparents and children, as well as between parents and the second or third spouses of their children. And sometimes parents and children enlist in one another's marital wars.

There are also broad shifts taking place in social values. The implicit understanding that children will take care of their of their aging parents is no longer a standard social value. Parents who sacrificed for their children may not be able to count on their children doing the same for them. And you, having raised your kids, probably remember well the parental burdens of your younger years. Your children, now with careers and children of their own to raise, face the same sort of demands you faced when you were young.

With much higher rates of divorce and remarriage, many retirees have stepchildren as well as biological children to think about.

New Family Opportunities

Despite the obstacles and potential pitfalls, families—like friendships—become increasingly important over time. As you shed your traditional job responsibilities and the tasks of child rearing, you have a chance to relax and take those relationships to a higher level.

In your retirement, you're being presented with some wonderful opportunities to know your children as adults, to be great friends with your grandkids, and, if your parents are still living, to enter a whole new phase with them. In addition, you may have the time and the inclination to start or renew relationships with other family members: siblings, nephews and nieces, cousins, and aunts and uncles. Your main focus, though, will likely be on your kids, your grandkids, and your parents.

As you shed your traditional job responsibilities and the tasks of child rearing, you have a chance to relax and take those relationships to a higher level.

Your Children

By the time you retire, or contemplate it, your children have probably left home and may already be parents themselves. Their climb to adulthood has already altered your relationship in many ways. You're no longer responsible for them. Usually, both you and they are independent. And, ideally at least, you and your kids can talk as equals.

As your children have grown into adulthood, your relationship with them has changed all along. But as you enter retirement, that relationship enters a new stage in its evolution. Now is a time, as with all relationships in your life, to reassess and renew your relationship. But as this relationship is built on a foundation of the past, it may well contain hurts and slights and mistakes and words uttered in anger. If this is the case, can you relearn how to talk to one another without letting the residue from the past interfere?

The first entry in this chapter will help you to think about your relationship with your children. Although you can use this as a general entry to write about all of your kids, you can also use the entry repeatedly to write about *each* child individually.

YOUR CHILDREN

1. Describe your relationship with your children.

_____

_____

_____

_____

2. If you have more than one child, in what ways does your relationship differ with each?

_____

_____

_____

_____

3. If you have more than one child, do you treat your children differently? How?

_____

_____

_____

_____

4. Do you treat your children in the way that you want to be treated by them?

_____

_____

_____

_____

5. How do you see your children? As responsible and capable, for example, or unreliable and incompetent?

_____

_____

_____

_____

_____

6. Do you feel you need to improve your relationship with any of your children? If so, why and in what way?

_____

_____

_____

_____

_____

7. Are you satisfied with your relationship with your children?

_____

_____

_____

_____

_____

8. Are your children satisfied with their relationship with you?

_____

_____

_____

_____

_____

9. When I think of my child/children, I . . . _____

_____

_____

_____

_____

THINGS TO THINK ABOUT

- Do you view your relationship with your kids as a plus or a minus?
- Would improving the relationship with your child/children bring you an added measure of security and/or contentment in retirement?
- Have you explained your retirement needs and wishes with your child/children? What are the risks of *not* having that talk?

Parent-Child Dialogue

One key to improving your relationship with your children before and during retirement is talking and, where necessary, getting the issues on the table. Try not to talk down to your children. Try to understand their lives and the pressures they live under. Try to help them separate what they do for you out of pleasure and what they do for you out of duty. Talk about each other's goals and how and if they mesh.

Now that both you and your children have grown up you have a different relationship, and with a different relationship comes different needs. What do you need from your kids, and what might they need from you? You might need their company at times, or their respect, concern, or financial help, and you might need to know that your children will care for you physically if you need help. You might simply need to know that they *want* you in their life and will remember you on birthdays and special occasions. They might need you to babysit the grandchildren, financial help

One key to improving your relationship with your children before and during retirement is talking and, where necessary, getting the issues on the table.

(that's a two-way street), or just to know that you can take care of yourself if needed. They might want you to talk to them and get their input *before* you make any major life decisions. They may just want to know that you value their ideas and their feelings.

In fact, your kids may well have strong reactions to your retirement decisions and behaviors. If you're widowed or divorced, for instance, how will your children respond if you begin to date or remarry? How will they respond if you decide to sell the family home and move across country? Do you know how they feel, and do you want to know? Perhaps their potential inheritance is an issue. Are they, for example, counting on it to educate their kids? Whatever the situation, the answers lie in communicating. Try to hash things out with your children. If you can't agree on every issue, that's okay, but at least try. That way each of you will get a better sense of where the other stands and can adjust your behavior.

Today's younger retirees face the real possibility of becoming the sandwich generation —caring for both their aging parents and their own grown children.

Taking Care of Your Children

Another retiree-child issue involves adult children who haven't found independence. With people living longer and good jobs for young people becoming harder to find, today's younger retirees face the real possibility of becoming the sandwich generation —caring for both their aging parents and their own grown children.

When grown children remain dependent, conflicts are unavoidable. On one hand, the retiree wants to be helpful; on the other hand, he or she doesn't want to be parenting forever. If the situation continues for long, there's bound to be resentment. So the reason for and length of the dependency become crucial.

If the child has had an accident and is unable to work, if he or she has suffered an emotional trauma (a bereavement or a divorce), or if a child has lost a job or had a serious financial setback, most parents would accept, even welcome, the chance to help out. But if the reason is less clear and the time frame open-ended, having a child move back in (or never move out) is likely to have serious repercussions. You need to remember that this is *your* retirement. While you probably want to help, you've also got to think of *your* needs. Besides, you're not doing your child a favor by tolerating an open-ended dependency.

TALKING TO YOUR KIDS

1. What do you want from your children in your postretirement relationship?

_____

_____

_____

_____

_____

2. What do you most need?

_____

_____

_____

_____

3. What about *mutuality* in your relationship?

a. What can your kids do for you? _____

_____

_____

b. What can you do for them? _____

_____

_____

4. Do your children understand what you want to do with your retirement? Have you told them?

_____

_____

_____

_____

_____

5. Do you know what your kids expect and want from you in your retirement? Have they told you? Have you asked them?

_____

_____

_____

_____

_____

6. Will you share your ideas and decisions with your children before you act on them? Does it matter to you what your kids think?

_____

_____

_____

_____

_____

7. How will you help your kids adjust to big changes in your life, such as a decision to move or remarry?

_____

_____

_____

_____

8. How can you best cope and deal with your changing relationship with your kids?

_____

_____

_____

_____

_____

9. What is the best possible relationship you can imagine having with your children?

_____

_____

_____

_____

_____

THINGS TO THINK ABOUT

- Parents often expect a lot from their grown children. What can *you* do to bring the best possible future relationship you described in Question 9?
- Do you need to talk with your kids more? Do you need to change the way you talk to them now?
- Are you optimistic or pessimistic about your future relationship with your kids?

Your Grandchildren

Grandchildren can be a marvelous tonic for the retiree, and often are. But in a world of divorce and working parents, there may be a bigger role for grandparents than in times past. It's been estimated that six million families depend on grandparents for primary child care. Is this a role you want to play? Does this fit with your own plans for how you want to spend your retirement days?

Whatever the family situation, for many retirees grandparenthood is a wonderful experience that provides reinvigoration and a terrific new outlet for your energy and attention even as your devotion to your job wanes. More than ever, grandparents are in a position to make a major difference in their grandchildren's lives.

Mentoring your grandchildren can be more enjoyable than raising your children. At its best, grandparenting is like raising children again, with the ability to enjoy the fun parts without the responsibility. But your role as grandparent is not as clearly defined as was your role as parent. Your relationship to your grandkids will probably hinge in large part on your relationship with their parents. If you don't enjoy warm relations with your children, you probably won't get close enough to the grandchildren to do any better with them.

Your role will also depend on what *you* want it to be—close or emotionally distant, sporadic or constant. Your relationship with the grandkids may even be impacted by the *other* set of grandparents. If they live closer or farther away, if they have more or less time, or if they prefer a different degree of intimacy with the grandkids, your role will probably be directly affected.

And, obviously, the closer you are, the more chances you have to be involved in your grandkids' lives. In short, there's a lot of moving parts in the grandparent-grandchild machinery. You're not a parent this time, and you're not in charge. So you need to be nimble and sensitive to these other considerations. Too much or too little attention to the grandchild can lead to simmering resentments.

Making the Most of Grandparenting

What's important to remember is that you want to be a problem solver, not a problem, when it comes to the grandkids.

- Be a helper, not an instructor. For instance, give the parents the day off by babysitting or having your grandkids spend

For many retirees grandparenthood is a wonderful experience that provides reinvigoration and a terrific new outlet for your energy and attention even as your devotion to your job wanes.

time with you. Help your children be the parents *they* want to be, not the parents *you* think they should be. Give help when asked, and offer it whenever possible, but make sure the help is wanted by the parents.

+ Develop a one-on-one relationship. Spend time with your grandchildren one at a time whenever possible, without their parents always there. In that way, you'll build a real relationship and a bond with your grandkids, and they will get to know you as a *person*.

+ Don't buy love. Grandkids love their grandparents to be, as one sociologist puts it, "a somewhat intermittent St. Nicholas." Grandparents buy one-fourth of all toys sold in the United States. But taken to extremes, this can cause conflicts with the parents and damage your relationship with the child, who may come to value your gifts more than you.

+ Spend active time together. Expand your grandkids' world by sharing your interests or theirs. Take them to a ball game or bowling, if that's your idea of fun, or go watch them in their school play or taking swimming lessons. Or have them help you with gardening, take them hiking, or do whatever it is that will allow the two of you to be active and get to know one another deeply.

+ Avoid obsession. If you live close to your grandkids and enjoy a warm relationship with them and their parents, consider yourself blessed. But don't make grandparenting your whole life. That's unhealthy and probably intrusive. Be actively involved, but don't be obsessive.

Remember your relationship with your own grandparents, and use that as a yardstick. If it was a good relationship, then you have an ideal model. If your grandparents were too close or too distant, too harsh or too lenient, you may get an idea for how you could develop your own role as a grandparent.

Expand your grandkids' world by sharing your interests or theirs.

You have a special opportunity with your grandchildren and a chance to mold that opportunity in whatever way you see fit. Take some time to plan your grandparenting to figure out what's best for them and you.

WHAT KIND OF A GRANDPARENT?

1. What kind of relationship do you want with your grandchildren? Check all that apply and add other answers of your own.

__babysitter	__confidant	__someone to pass the time with
__bearer of gifts	__head of the family	__substitute parent
__bridge to the family's traditions	__mentor	__teacher
__buddy	__playmate	__wise elder

other:_____   _____

_____   _____

2. What do want your grandchildren to be for *you*?

__a fresh burst of enthusiasm for living   __an antidote to loneliness

__second chance to raise a child   __someone to give you unconditional love

__someone you can love   __someone to pass the time with

other:_____   _____

_____   _____

_____   _____

3. What family values and traditions do you want to pass on to your grandkids?

_____

_____

_____

_____

4. What's the best way to do that?

_____

_____

_____

_____

5. What are the special resources you bring to grandparenting?

_____

_____

_____

_____

6. What might be your greatest contribution to the growth and development of your grandchildren?

_____

_____

_____

_____

7. What's the best way to spend time with your grandchildren?

_____

_____

_____

_____

8. How can you have the most fun together?

_____

_____

_____

_____

9. Looking back at your answers to Questions 1 and 2, do *your* needs match the needs and best interests of your grandchildren?

_____

_____

_____

_____

_____

THINGS TO THINK ABOUT

- How does being a grandparent fit with your retirement plans? Do you want to play an active role as a grandparent?
- How will you deal with a smaller grandparenting role than you might otherwise prefer? How will you deal with more demands than you would prefer?
- Can you be an involved grandparent in a way that's not threatening to the parents? Do your needs and ideas clash with those of the parents?

Taking Care of Your Grandchildren

More than four million American children live permanently with their grandparents, according to the American Association of Retired Persons (AARP).

The number of grandparents raising children in the United States is increasing because of broken families, single teenage mothers, drug-addicted parents, or parents who have died or divorced. In fact, more than four million American children live permanently with their grandparents, according to the American Association of Retired Persons (AARP). Because many of these grandparents are on fixed incomes and receive little help from government agencies, inconvenience and hardship can result.

If grandparents are available to raise children, they often provide a more stable, healthy environment than some of the alternatives, such as foster homes. A truly warm and loving relationship may result. However, the situation creates issues for both the grandchild and the grandparent. These can include anger by the child toward his or her biological parents, extreme age disparity with the grandparents, or the child's inability to cope with the aging of the grandparent.

Similarly, the situation is mixed for the grandparent. The presence of children in the home may keep loneliness and isolation at bay, but it also can be annoying and may complicate their relationship with their real children. The grandchild may be a physical, financial, and emotional burden, and the grandparent may have anger toward the parent for not being capable or desirous of raising the child. And the retiree may not have a real chance to be retired at all.

As the emotional history of your past affects your current relationship with your children, the past also colors your relationship with your parents.

Your Parents

It can be very nice, as you approach retirement, to have a parent or parents, but it can also be a significant burden. Obviously, if the aging parent is ill, that brings a whole set of problems and emotions. Affection and obligation become entwined. But even when the parent is reasonably well and independent, age inevitably means increasing dependence.

Just as the emotional history of your past affects your current relationship with your children, the past also colors your relationship with *your* parents. But now it's you who has to overcome childhood wounds. As with your children, communication is important here. Try to discuss issues with your parents while they're independent and healthy, and make sure that you also discuss the challenges of the future.

For example, what should be done if your parents become ill and extremely dependent? What are their preferences about nursing homes, live-in care, and other arrangements? Are their affairs in order, or do they need help with that? And what can you do *now* to add pleasure or meaning to their lives? Most important, understand their need for emotional support. You can't prevent the setbacks and losses your parents will experience as they age and face their illnesses and the loss of their friends, just as *your* children can't protect you from these inevitable realities. But you can cushion their effect by listening, caring, and being there for them when they're sad or depressed.

Above all, remember that even when we care a great deal about someone, we often fail to say so. Tell your parents what they mean to you, how you appreciate all they've done for you, and encourage them to have good feelings about their lives. See their changing status, and your own, as an opportunity to draw closer to them and allow them to become closer to you. In short, make the most of your relationship with your parents. They're the only parents you'll ever have.

But once again, a sense of balance is needed. You want to listen to, care for, and be there for them, but you've also got to live your own life. For your emotional health and theirs, you must avoid becoming overly involved.

Taking Care of Yourself

If you have to care for grown children, grandchildren, or your parents, it's natural that you may have some anger because your retirement plans probably didn't take this into account. Giving such care can be stressful, physically and emotionally.

- Look for causes. If you're allowing your life to be dictated by your child, grandchild, or parents, ask yourself why. Perhaps the situation really is unavoidable, but maybe you're being overly responsible and don't need to carry all the weight. Understanding the causes of any problems always offers the possibility of finding more than one solution.

- Set limits. You need to protect your own physical and emotional health, as well as your retirement. Think about and establish limits about what you can and *will* do, what you can't and *won't* do, and how long a situation can be allowed to persist. See if you can get other relatives to help shoulder the load.

- Allow yourself to have limits. Accept your own limitations, and don't be a perfectionist. You can't fix all problems all of the time, and you shouldn't have to. Not everyone involved, including you, is going to be happy all the time. Accept that fact and with it your own limitations as a caregiver and fixer of problems.

- Ask for help. You not only can ask other relatives for money, time, and support, but you can also investigate social agencies and nonprofit groups that may aid people in your situation. Many social services and senior-assistance referral lines are listed in your Yellow Pages.

Think about and establish limits about what you can and will *do, what you can't and won't* do, *and how long a situation can be allowed to persist.*

An Opportunity to Draw Closer

Your retirement offers a wonderful opportunity not only for the relaxation, leisure, and personal development that you've been thinking and writing about as you work your way through *The Healing Journey Through Retirement,* but also the revisiting, development, and deepening of family relationships and ties across the generations.

Think about what you want from your family relationships *and* how to best use this time and best ensure that your retirement meets your own needs as fully and completely as possible.

12

Destination:

LOOKING TO THE PAST

TRISHA

It was pretty odd reaching retirement age. I felt good about not having to work again, but also felt afraid that I'd have nothing to do and I'd waste away. My only models for retirement were my own parents, and they didn't do much with their lives after work stopped for them. I'd always remembered what my father had said to me a couple of years after he retired, and I worried I'd feel the same way. He said that once retired, every day was the same as every other. That was an important memory for me because it was such a pessimistic thing to say and feel. I never forgot what he said, and that memory actually helped me become that much more determined to have every day of my *retirement feel like a holiday and* not *just another day. Who would ever have thought that a memory from the past like that could help shape my own future?*

YOUR RETIREMENT IS a milestone that marks a lifetime of work accomplished. It is a turning point in your life, separating what was from what will be. And one way to better understand where you're going is to look back at where you've been. Look-

223

ing back into your own past can help you clearly see the path you took to get where you are today and the path to take as you enter the future.

Looking back can be an exercise in nostalgia and possibly regret. But in the spirit of your retirement, which is after all a celebration, looking back means exploring and remembering a life fully lived. In order to best understand yourself and what you'll take with you into your own future, you have to be able to glance backward, perhaps not without some regret, but with acceptance and satisfaction.

In this chapter, you'll have an opportunity to look back at your own life and create a biography. And like all memoirs, this will be a *living* autobiography that begins in your past but continues to grow each day as you live your life and pass into you future. Indeed, for many people, it is the creation and development of the memoir and the chronicling of life history that is the most satisfying aspect of journaling.

In the spirit of your retirement, looking back means exploring and remembering a life fully lived. In order to best understand yourself and what you'll take with you into your own future, you have to be able to glance backward.

Looking Back

Not everybody looks back at their life with pleasure. Not everything has gone just the way it should have gone, and not everyone has accomplished all those things they hoped they would. As people age, they begin to compare themselves with others their own age and begin to feel as though time is slipping away. But, regardless of how well you've accomplished earlier tasks, succeeded in earlier relationships, or met career or other personal goals, you have a whole life ahead of you. Here, the past is prologue. You have an opportunity to look back and learn from your own history, good and bad, just who it is you are and who you want to become. You have the opportunity to celebrate a life lived and a life still in the making.

What do you see when you look back? What do you remember, and what do you feel? There are many who look back at the past with regret or whose recollections are sad or disturbing. Some people see the past as their best days, when things were so much better or somehow more full of life. Others have fond recollections of their past but still live happily in the present. They have, perhaps, been the most successful at using good experiences as builders of self-esteem and using not-so-good memories as character builders or lessons learned.

THROUGH THE PAST LIGHTLY

1. *The past set the stage for my present life by . . .* _____

_____

_____

_____

2. *The past was instructional because . . .* _____

_____

_____

_____

3. *The past gave me . . .* _____

_____

_____

_____

4. *The past took from me . . .* _____

_____

_____

_____

5. *When I think of my past, I . . .* _____

_____

_____

_____

6. *About myself, my past has taught me . . .* _____

_____

_____

_____

7. *My past was . . .* _____

_____

_____

_____

8. What have you learned from your past?

_____

_____

_____

9. How have you benefited from your past?

_____

_____

_____

THINGS TO THINK ABOUT

- Is there a theme in what you've written? Do you see your past as a powerful tool or something to get away from?
- Was it difficult to find answers to these questions or complete the sentences? Were all your answers meaningful to you? What have you learned about yourself?
- Do you spend much time thinking about your past? Is it possible to spend too much time thinking about the past?

Markers and Milestones

Some moments in your past are far more memorable than others, and some are more influential. Some of these become markers in your life, signifying or highlighting important changes, or milestones, which tell you how far you've come or how far you have to go.

Sometimes these landmarks are people, events, or things that happened to you. Relationships often stand as markers or milestones, such as a first romance, a marriage, or an important friendship. Sometimes it's the person more than the relationship that counts—perhaps a parent or an uncle or aunt, a high-school teacher, or a teammate, someone who you looked up to or who affected your life in a powerful way. Other markers or milestones are things, like graduating junior high, winning a competition, going on to college, leaving home, or your first job. As you're *still* developing, there will continue to be markers and milestones in your life. Indeed, your retirement itself is an important marker, and if you've already retired, it already has become a landmark and a significant part of your history.

Your history involves those formative moments and events that stand out, and from which your character was and is built. People and events that shake, shape, or affect your life in some way are more than just important events in your past; they become important moments in your *history*. In order to make use of our history, we have to first remember it.

In the next journal entry, think back to important landmarks in your history—those things that contributed to who you are today or seemed to point the way. Landmarks can reside in your deep memory, dating back to early childhood, or they can be as recent as yesterday. It's not *when* they happened, but their impact on your life. Although the entry begins with a series of people, relationships, and events, it finally focuses on only one landmark, so you may want to photocopy this entry for repeated use.

Some moments in your past are far more memorable than others, and some are more influential. Some of these become markers in your life, signifying or highlighting important changes, or milestones, which tell you how far you've come or how far you have to go.

LANDMARKS

1. Name five important people in your life.

Person	Your Age	His or Her Importance
_____	____	_____
_____	____	_____
_____	____	_____
_____	____	_____
_____	____	_____

2. Name five important relationships.

Relationship	Your Age	Significance
_____	____	_____
_____	____	_____
_____	____	_____
_____	____	_____
_____	____	_____

3. Name five important events.

Event	Your Age	Importance
_____	____	_____
_____	____	_____
_____	____	_____
_____	____	_____
_____	____	_____

4. Pick one of these people, relationships, or events and focus on it for the remainder of the entry.

_____

5. Some events or people in your life are *markers,* reminding you of important changes or moments. Others are *milestones,* which tell you how far you've come or how far you

have to go. Is the landmark you've picked for this entry more like a marker or a mile-stone? Why?

_____

_____

_____

_____

_____

6. How was this a shaping or important landmark?

_____

_____

_____

_____

_____

7. Looking back, how have you changed? Have you changed?

_____

_____

_____

_____

_____

8. Who are you as a result of your history?

_____

_____

_____

_____

_____

The Past as Prologue

Some aspects of your past reside not only in your mind, but also in things that capture and remind you of your history. Take a look into your past. Spend an evening looking at old photos, slides, videotapes, or home movies of yourself and your family. If you're a keeper of old letters or if you kept diaries back then, pull them out and read back through them. If you have other memorabilia, such as awards, trophies, or mementos, take a tour of them. If you're married or in a committed relationship, sift through these memories with your partner. As you look back, think about what you can learn about your life from these memorabilia and how much your life has changed. What were you doing for work, and how did work fit—or *not* fit—into your life back then? How did it affect and shape your life in those days? How have you changed? If you have a family, how has it changed? What things were important to you, and are they still?

When you've completed this look back into your past, think about how it's affected your thinking about the present and the future. Then complete the next entry, using it to describe your thoughts and reflect upon the experience.

A LOOK BACK

1. What was striking about this experience of looking back into your past?

_____

_____

_____

_____

_____

2. What's no longer important, but once was?

_____

_____

_____

_____

3. What's important now, but never used to be?

_____

_____

_____

_____

4. What was important then and now?

_____

_____

_____

_____

5. What have you lost over these years?

_____

_____

_____

6. What have you gained?

_____

_____

_____

_____

7. What do you most miss?

_____

_____

_____

_____

8. What would you now most like to give up?

_____

_____

_____

_____

9. What have you learned from your look back?

_____

_____

_____

_____

THINGS TO THINK ABOUT

- Is it important to look back into history to better understand your present and how you got here?
- As you think about your life now compared to your life as it was, ask yourself if this is the way you want it to be? Does it have to be this way?
- If you shared this history with your spouse, what sort of extra dimension was added?

Special Days

There are many reasons to look back on your history: the recollection of friends and family, good and sad times, turning points in your life, and the memory of lessons learned that help you in your life today. Among all the days of your life, there are also those days and times that stand out as special, days not easily forgotten.

These days are enormously important, if only because they remain so clear in memory. In some cases, they're the good days—the fun times, the accomplishments, the special event or celebration. In other cases, the memories aren't so good—a bad experience, a shattered dream or dashed hope, a disappointment, or sad news. For the next entry, think of days that stand out in your memory. Each day can be important for any number of reasons: It could be a fun day or an awful one. It could be a milestone for you or for another member of your family, or it could be a day that simply stands out because of the weather or where you happened to be. The day could be momentous, or just a fast-food meal with a friend. It doesn't matter if it's a memory of a good day or a difficult time. What counts here is that the day has significance to you for some reason.

AN IMPORTANT DAY

1. List at least six important good days.

_____   _____

_____   _____

_____   _____

_____   _____

_____   _____

2. List at least six important bad days.

_____   _____

_____   _____

_____   _____

_____   _____

_____   _____

3. Pick one of these days—good or bad—as the focus of this journal entry. You can repeat the entry again for each of the other days on your list.

_____

4. Describe this important day.

_____

_____

_____

_____

_____

_____

5. Who were you with on this particular day?

_____

_____

_____

6. Was the person you were with part of what made this day important? If so, why?

_____

_____

_____

7. I chose to write about this day because . . . _____

_____

_____

8. This day is important in my history because . . . _____

_____

_____

_____

9. As I think of this day, it makes me feel . . . _____

_____

_____

_____

THINGS TO THINK ABOUT

- What was it like to recall this day? How did it leave you feeling?
- Is there a lesson learned from this day?
- Is it important to remember these days? Will you write about the other special days in your history?
- Are there people in your current life with whom you should count every day as important?

An Autobiography

An autobiography is a personal memoir. It's you writing about you. As you work through *The Healing Journey Through Retirement*, you're creating an autobiography of sorts. Your journal contains your ideas, thoughts, feelings, and concerns, and memories of your past and visions of your future. A *formal* autobiography or memoir usually has a particular slant or direction and a focus on a specific aspect of the life being chronicled.

Use the next journal entry to create a focused autobiographical sketch of your life, taking only ten minutes to do so. As people are complex beings with rich lives and histories, it's inconceivable that a brief autobiography can do much more than create

A formal autobiography or memoir usually has a particular slant or direction and a focus on a specific aspect of the life being chronicled.

a character sketch of one aspect of your life. And, because the way you see yourself no doubt varies from day to day and may be influenced by your mood or recent events in your life, a ten-minute autobiography is likely to capture something important about how you see yourself *at the time you wrote it*. In other words, a short autobiographical sketch is just as likely to teach you something about yourself right now as it is to capture some aspect of your past.

Time yourself for this entry and take only ten minutes. If you like the idea of an autobiography and want to take more time, do that later. Right now, concentrate on the goal of a ten-minute autobiography. You can describe your life in any way you want. You can focus on your whole life, a single interval in it, or even a single incident. You can write a brief chronological account of your life, or you can shape your autobiography around a theme (for instance, strong influences on your life, memories you've never forgotten, or members of your family). This is a free-form journal entry with little structure to guide you other than the task itself.

Allow yourself five minutes to think about what you want to write about and how you're going to write it, then begin writing.

A TEN-MINUTE AUTOBIOGRAPHY

Day: _____ Date: _____

1. After five minutes of thought and planning, write your autobiography. Time yourself, and write for only ten minutes.

_____

_____

_____

_____

_____

2. What does your autobiography reflect about today—the moment and circumstances surrounding you as you wrote it? Was the style, subject matter, or theme influenced by today in some way?

_____

_____

_____

_____

_____

_____

_____

3. If you had to write another autobiography, would you focus on the same subject matter and simply write it from another perspective, or would you choose another slice of or look at your life?

_____

_____

_____

_____

_____

_____

THINGS TO THINK ABOUT

- Look back at your autobiography. What does it say about you? Does it offer an optimistic, upbeat view of who you are? Does it reflect a sense of high self-esteem, low self-esteem, indifference, or detachment?
- Did you discover anything important about yourself? Does your autobiography somehow reflect how you feel about yourself in general?
- Was the mood reflected in the autobiography determined or shaped by events in your present life?

Another Autobiography

In the previous entry, you wrote a ten-minute autobiography. Now look at yourself and your history through a different lens. Pick a *different* day and write another ten-minute autobiography. Only this time, include *none* of the same material described in your first autobiography.

Again, you can describe your life in any way you want. You can describe your whole life, an interval in your life, or a single incident. You can shape your autobiography on a theme or you can try a free-flowing autobiography. But include *none* of the material from your previous autobiography.

As always, this is a journal entry that can be repeated over and over. In this way, if you choose, you can build a complete autobiography of your life through a collection of short essay-style autobiographies that not only record your life as it *was,* but your life as it *is* at the time of writing.

ANOTHER TEN-MINUTE AUTOBIOGRAPHY

Day: _____ Date: _____

1. After five minutes of thought and planning, write your additional autobiography. Time yourself, and write for only ten minutes.

_____

_____

_____

_____

_____

_____

_____

2. How is this second autobiography different from the first one?

_____

_____

_____

3. *Why* is this autobiography different?

_____

_____

_____

_____

4. Would people reading the two autobiographies realize they were reading about the same person? How?

_____

_____

_____

_____

5. What influenced your choice of material or style for this autobiography?

_____

_____

_____

_____

THINGS TO THINK ABOUT

- How are your two biographies related? Together, taken as a whole, what do they say about you as a person?
- Was it difficult or simple to write this second autobiography? Did you discover anything different about yourself?
- Have you learned anything about yourself by writing these biographies? Could you write a third autobiography? Will you?

The Living Autobiography

Writing is a form of self-expression that can help you clarify your thinking and express your feelings, talk to yourself, and capture your life and times on paper.

Writing is a form of self-expression that can help you clarify your thinking and express your feelings, talk to yourself, and capture your life and times on paper.

The next journal entry provides a format for a daily journal entry, and thus a living autobiography. This is a simple entry that you can use to unload your thoughts and feelings, describe your day, and record what you're going through as part of your personal history. If you decide to use this format daily, make sure you copy the blank before using it for the first time. At the end of the entry, add a thought for the day. This can be anything that impresses, inspires, or strikes you or is in some way worth remembering. Finding a thought for each day pushes you to look outside of yourself, even as you find ways to express what's inside.

A DAILY DIARY

When I write down my thoughts, they do not escape me. This action makes me remember my strength."
— ISIDORE DUCASSE

Day: _____ Date: _____

1. What were the most pressing issues on your mind today?

_____

_____

_____

2. What special tasks, events, or incidents stand out?

_____

_____

_____

_____

3. What did you accomplish today?

_____

_____

_____

_____

_____

4. In general, how were you affected by this day?

_____

_____

_____

_____

_____

5. What's changing over time? Are issues getting resolved or building up?

_____

_____

_____

_____

6. What's going right?

_____

_____

_____

_____

7. *Today I'm feeling . . .* _____

_____

_____

_____

_____

8. *I want/need to say . . .* _____

_____

_____

_____

9. Other reflections on the day or this time in your life:

_____

_____

_____

_____

Thought for the day

_____

_____

_____

_____

THINGS TO THINK ABOUT

- Are the days going well? What can you do to increase the chances that they'll keep improving?
- Are there difficult days ahead? If so, how can you best prepare for them, and what support do you need?
- Are there things pressing for you that need your attention? What will happen if they don't get your attention?

Drawing from the Well

Revisiting the past is often an important experience for many reasons: sometimes just for nostalgia, and other times to work things out or complete unfinished business. Journals are not only great places to record your current life and your march into the future, they also provide a wonderful way to think back on your life and consider the relevance of what *was* to what *is*. If looking back at your past has been useful in making sense of your present, you may want to continue this reflective glance.

The journal entries in this chapter have provided specific ways to focus your thinking on your history, but there are dozens of ways to look back on and write about the past. These include repeating or modifying the structured journal entries provided in this chapter or simply writing about specific incidents, experiences, or people that stand out as important.

The final entry in this chapter provides a means for self-affirmation and celebration of who you are. An affirmation is an assertion of a truth, a belief, or an ideal—a way to put out an idea and commit yourself to it. In this case, the affirmation reflects your commitment to *yourself*—your own health, goodness, strength, and ability to make the best use of this time in your life.

Journals are not only great places to record your current life and your march into the future, they also provide a wonderful way to think back on your life and consider the relevance of what was to what is.

CELEBRATING YOURSELF

I. Name at least four things in your life of which you're proud. These can include things you've accomplished, children you've parented, relationships you've had, musical instruments you've learned to play, special skills or abilities you've developed, challenges or adversity you've overcome, or decisions you've made.

a. _____

b. _____

c. _____

d. _____

e. _____

f. _____

2. Now describe at least four personal qualities about which you can feel good. These can include your generosity, your intellect, your sense of humor, your organizational

skills, your creativity, your compassion for issues or empathy for others, your ability to make new friends, your attitudes and beliefs, or any other quality you choose.

a. _____

b. _____

c. _____

d. _____

e. _____

f. _____

3. Complete these sentences.

a. *Even though there are always things to feel bad about, I . . .* _____

_____

_____

_____

b. *Although I'm experiencing changes that are new to me, I . . .* _____

_____

_____

_____

_____

c. *I draw strength from . . .* _____

_____

_____

_____

_____

d. *Above all I value myself because . . .* _____

_____

_____

_____

e. *One thought that helps me through difficult times is . . .* _____

_____

_____

_____

THINGS TO THINK ABOUT

- Was this a difficult entry for you—were you able to describe accomplishments or personal qualities of which you're proud? If not, why not?
- Do self-reinforcing thoughts help you gather internal strength or feel better about yourself during a difficult time?
- Will it be useful to focus on a self-affirming thought every day?

13

Destination:

PLANNING AHEAD

"If one advances confidently in the direction of his dreams and endeavors to live the life that he has imagined, he will meet with a success unexpected in common hours."

——HENRY DAVID THOREAU

LEONARD

After practicing as a psychiatrist for years, I eventually came to find work numbing. I'd poured my heart into my work with my patients, and I focused my energy on their needs rather than on my own hopes and needs. After a lot of thought, I decided it was not only time to retire, but also time to ensure my retirement would be more stimulating than my job had become over the years.

Although I wasn't really ready to retire yet, I started thinking about what I'd really enjoyed when I was younger. I decided that it was time to get back to an old passion for art, something I was never able to indulge during my career. Even though I was still seeing patients, I took some art appreciation courses, and I went on to take beginning and advanced painting classes. I visited galleries and attended openings and read more and more about art. I used some of the contacts I'd made during my years as a psychiatrist, and through them and my classes made several friends and acquaintances in the art world and got invited to artists' social gatherings. By the time I was ready to give up my practice, I'd earned a spot on the board of

directors of a university museum and bought into a small gallery. Once retired, I never looked back. Actually, I feel like I've been reborn and love the role art plays in my retired life.

YOU'RE BY NOW in the final stages of *your* journey through retirement. In this journal, you've had the opportunity to think about your retirement and the role it plays in your life now and in shaping your future. But retirement isn't a singular thing any more than your career was. Retirement is just a word that describes the state of your life. Although you'll always be retired, your life will continue to change, and you will continue to grow. For this reason, like most of life's journey, your journey through retirement doesn't really have an endpoint or a final destination.

Retirement is just a word that describes the state of your life. Although you'll always be retired, your life will continue to change, and you will continue to grow.

Life has been described by some as a management problem. First, you have to decide where you want to go, then you have to figure out how to get there. That's probably never more true than in retirement, when how you spend your time is largely up to you. Suddenly, you have the means to do as you please, but maybe not a goal. At best, that's a recipe for boredom, at worst, unhappiness and even serious depression. "The tragedy of life is not death," Norman Cousin wrote, "rather, it is what we allow to die within ourselves while we live."

The Toughest Questions of All

Successful retirement involves, in large part, making effective decisions. And before you can plan the rest of your life, you need to know where you are now and where you want to be. This involves asking yourself the sorts of questions that aren't usually discussed on the golf course, at cocktail parties, or even with your spouse. But you're at a watershed period in your life, and the questions need to be asked and answered. You're entering a new territory, with no one to lead you through it but yourself. If you've reached this chapter after working through *The Healing Journey Through Retirement,* then you've thought, written about, and addressed many of the issues involved in making a successful transition from the workforce to retirement.

Do you know where your retirement journey is taking you? As you complete the next journal entry, consider whether you're ready to make some of the decisions that lie just ahead. If you find it difficult to answer some of these questions, then you may not be ready to move on with any significant decisions. It's time to state a basic safety rule: It's usually a poor idea to make decisions when you're under a great deal of pressure or following sudden life changes. The word of caution is to move slowly and not behave or make decisions impetuously.

REVIEWING YOUR PATH

1. What would you like to accomplish in the years ahead of you?

_____

_____

_____

_____

_____

2. What's really important to you? If you knew you had but a few weeks or months to live, how would you use them?

_____

_____

_____

_____

_____

3. Are you living the life you want to live, or are you following a script written by yourself or someone else years ago? If it's the latter, what is that script, and do you want to change it?

_____

_____

_____

_____

_____

4. Are you spending your present time wisely? Are you moving along the path you want to move along?

_____

_____

_____

_____

_____

5. What is missing the most from your life right now?

_____

_____

_____

_____

_____

6. What do you *most* need to do in order to prepare for any changes that may lie ahead?

_____

_____

_____

_____

_____

Decisions and Choices

Some things *never* change. As always, your life is full of decisions and, more to the point, full of choices. In some ways, making decisions about your life can be summed up this simply: As your life is changing or has already changed, where do you want to be, what do you want to be doing, and who do you want to be doing it with? No doubt, you face and are limited by many constraints —family, relationships, finances, health, and other things over which you don't necessarily have full control. These make up the backdrop of your life against which decisions are made. Within that context, there's usually no way to advise you of the "correct" decision, or the "right" course to take. In fact, there's often more than one "correct" decision, and more than one "wrong" choice. But there are certainly guides to decision making that can help you think about and arrive at an *appropriate* decision.

Making decisions about your life can be summed up this simply: As your life is changing or has already changed, where do you want to be, what do you want to be doing, and who do you want to be doing it with?

As you consider your choices and think about appropriate decisions, consider the fact that most of your choices have consequences, certainly for yourself and possibly for others. As you think about decisions and your choices, consider these three factors:

- *Responsibility.* Some decisions are really *requirements.* If you're a parent of young or teenage children, for instance, you have decisions that must be made to ensure their health and safety. Similarly, if you have elderly parents who depend on you for care and financial support, you have obligations that limit the amount of flexibility you may have in decision making. Consequently, as you think about your choices, think about who will be affected by your decisions as you plan for and move into your future.

+ *Spontaneity versus impetuousness.* Sometimes there's no reason not to act on a whim or make a quick choice. Actually, it's healthy to be spontaneous at times. On the other hand, acting without thinking can be foolhardy if the consequences are not considered. Where spontaneity is usually thought of as harmless and even refreshing, impetuous behavior is usually seen as thoughtless and problematic. As you make decisions, think about the difference between being spontaneous and being impetuous. Decisions that affect your life and the lives of others should be carefully considered.

+ *Long-term effects.* Finally, take into account that decisions you make now may have effects that stay with you a long time. Buying a new wardrobe of clothes, seeking a new career, or moving to a new home in the same community may involve some deep decision making, but none represent radical change. On the other hand, selling your home and moving to another state, leaving your spouse, or investing your life's savings in a new business venture are far more significant decisions in terms of their long-term impact, and such decisions are often difficult to later reverse.

DECISIONS AND CHOICES

1. Think about *current* decisions and choices in your life. What kinds of decisions are the hardest to make?

_____

_____

_____

_____

_____

2. In what way has your retirement contributed or led directly to the sorts of choices you're facing?

_____

_____

_____

_____

_____

3. In what ways has retirement opened up the possibility of change?

_____

_____

_____

_____

_____

4. What sorts of opportunities for change are in your life right now?

_____

_____

_____

_____

5. What are the risks of change?

_____

_____

_____

_____

_____

6. Who else will be affected by your decisions, and in what ways?

_____

_____

_____

_____

_____

THINGS TO THINK ABOUT

- Are you afraid of change or excited by it? Do your fears about change outweigh the opportunities?
- Are you at a point in your life where you can spot opportunity for change? What can you do to increase your ability to see such opportunities?

Moving Forward

Is moving on simply a matter of a new attitude, a shift in the things you do, or a restructuring of your life?

What sorts of choices are you facing now as you move forward, and what kinds of decisions are you making? Are you deciding to make no immediate changes, or are you considering major changes in your life or relationships? Is moving on simply a matter of a new attitude, a shift in the things you do, or a restructuring of your life? If you have the freedom to make decisions without regard for anyone or anything else (such as kids, spouse, or financial obligations), are you thinking about changing jobs, going back to school, traveling the world, or moving across country?

Although there is no right or wrong here, there are steps that can help you to arrive at decisions that are appropriate for your lifestyle and responsibilities.

- The first step is recognizing that you do have choices. Much of the time, you're not simply a product of the way things have to be.

- Consider the nature of the problem that you're trying to resolve. Every decision is a *response* to a particular situation: What's the issue, problem, or situation you want to address?

- Think of all the possible choices you have in this case. Think of every possible choice, including the outlandish ones. In this step, your job is to be creative—what decisions *could* be made?

- Evaluate your choices. Now think about those choices that you can realistically make right now in light of your life. If only one choice comes up, you may even come up with a clear decision at this point.

- Consequences. What are the downsides of your possible choices? Who will be affected by your choice and how? How will your choices affect your life, finances, relationships, and so on?

- Reflection. Think about the decision you're planning to make: What will it feel like to actually take those steps and make that choice? What will it feel like to *not* make that choice? Is the decision you're pondering permanent, or is it reversible?

The next journal entry is intended to help you think about individual choices, as well as your decision-making style in general. Copy the blank format if you think you may want to repeat the entry to think through the same decision from more than one perspective.

Follow the general model for decision making described above. This is a framework you can use to think about and map out solutions for almost any issue in your life, from relationship choices to decisions about changes in your lifestyle.

MAKING DECISIONS

1. Briefly describe one decision you're currently pondering.

_____

_____

_____

_____

_____

2. Name at least six different ways to resolve this issue.

_____

_____

_____

3. Review the possible choices you've just identified, and select the three most realistic choices. Under each, describe how this choice could fit the circumstances and reality of your life.

a. *This solution fits because* . . . _____

b. *This solution fits because* . . . _____

c. *This solution fits because* . . . _____

4. Now, select just one of these choices and use it as the focal point for the remainder of this entry. You might want to repeat this entry several times in order to think through each of the possible choices you identified.

_____

5. What are possible consequences of this choice? Is there a price to pay?

_____

_____

_____

_____

_____

6. How will your life be affected by this choice?

_____

_____

_____

_____

_____

7. Who else's life will be affected by this decision, and how?

_____

_____

_____

_____

_____

THINGS TO THINK ABOUT

- Do you better understand the issues and choices involved in this decision? What stops you from making a choice and acting on it in this case?
- Can you afford to take a chance on this decision, or are the consequences irreversible?
- Are you acting too quickly on decisions without giving them ample thought, or are you not acting quickly enough? Are you discussing the issues and choices with your spouse, other family members, or friends? If not, why not?

To Move or Not to Move

For many retirees, moving is a very real and major issue. Your present home, especially if you've lived there for some time, may well be very comfortable for you — psychologically, as well as physically and financially.

For many retirees, moving is a very real and major issue. It's also a very individual matter, as we each have a different history, needs, and habits. Your present home, especially if you've lived there for some time, may well be very comfortable for you — psychologically, as well as physically and financially.

Your home may be filled with many wonderful memories. The surrounding environment, with its familiar streets or sights, is a known part of your geographic and emotional landscape. Friends and family may live nearby, and there may be an economic incentive to staying put, such as a low mortgage payment or no mortgage at all. If where you live now is comfortable and affordable, fills other needs, and isn't too large or difficult to manage, why move? Perhaps in this case, your best bet is to stay put. But for some retirees, there are many reasons to move: a better climate, closer to family or friends, new sights, a change of pace, a community geared to an older population, or a smaller or more economically or physically manageable home. Perhaps a move is prompted by a family member who is putting pressure on you to think about giving up your current home. If you've been thinking about moving, for any reason, the next journal entry can help you put your thoughts into perspective.

TO MOVE?

1. Is moving something you've been considering? If so, why?

_____

_____

_____

_____

2. Is moving something you *want* to do, or do you feel you *must* move?

_____

_____

_____

_____

_____

_____

_____

_____

3. What are the advantage and disadvantages of staying where you are?

a. Advantages: _____

_____

_____

_____

b. Disadvantages: _____

_____

_____

_____

4. What would be some of the advantages and disadvantages of moving?

a. Advantages: _____

_____

_____

_____

b. Disadvantages: _____

_____

_____

_____

5. What do you want or need in a living community, and how important are these same amenities to your spouse? Check off all areas that are important to each of you, and rate the importance of each item.

	Important to You			Important to Spouse		
	Not	Somewhat	Very	Not	Somewhat	Very
affordable cost of living	1	2	3	1	2	3
arts and culture	1	2	3	1	2	3
close to church or temple	1	2	3	1	2	3
clubs and community associations	1	2	3	1	2	3
entertainment	1	2	3	1	2	3
family nearby	1	2	3	1	2	3
friends nearby	1	2	3	1	2	3
low crime	1	2	3	1	2	3
medical facilities	1	2	3	1	2	3
minimal home upkeep	1	2	3	1	2	3
opportunity for community involvement	1	2	3	1	2	3
other retirees in community	1	2	3	1	2	3
planned group activities	1	2	3	1	2	3
pleasant climate	1	2	3	1	2	3
public transit	1	2	3	1	2	3
recreation and sports	1	2	3	1	2	3
restaurants	1	2	3	1	2	3
scenery or physical environment	1	2	3	1	2	3
shopping proximity	1	2	3	1	2	3
other:_____	1	2	3	1	2	3
_____	1	2	3	1	2	3
_____	1	2	3	1	2	3

6. Looking at the list you just created, are your needs and interests compatible with those of your spouse?

_____

_____

_____

_____

_____

7. How well does your present living situation meet the needs and interests you named in Question 5?

_____

_____

_____

_____

_____

8. If you move, what will you be leaving behind that you'll miss?

_____

_____

_____

_____

_____

9. If you move, what will you be gaining?

_____

_____

_____

_____

_____

- Do you want to further consider moving at this time? Is moving something you *want* to do, or are you feeling pressured to move? Conversely, do you want to move, but others want you to stay put?
- What has this entry helped you realize about *where* you want to live, or the type of community in which you want to live?
- If your needs are different from those of your partner, how will you address and resolve these differences?

Beginning Your Planning Process

Putting your ideas on paper is the real beginning of the planning process.

Planning, of course, involves thinking. But for the thinking to really take root, you must continue to write down your thoughts. Writing down your thoughts and feelings gives them a certain solidity and a degree of commitment. They're no longer just fleeting impulses, but something more tangible that you can see, shape, review, and revise. Putting your ideas on paper is the real beginning of the planning process.

To get started with a specific plan, you need specific goals. One way to get started is to buy a large loose-leaf binder with index tabs and assign a major life topic to each section. Start thinking about your potential goals within each topic area, and begin collecting information on each topic or goal, which could include:

- Finances
- Physical Health
- Travel
- Educational
- Vocational

- Emotional Health
- Spirituality
- Home

This notebook can be the building block for your pre- or post-retirement planning. Leave a few pages blank so that you can add other topics as they occur to you. Staple a large envelope on the divider pages to hold papers or clippings pertaining to each of the categories, and add magazine articles, newspaper clippings, sticky notes, or other memory joggers to each envelope. If you have a spouse or partner, ask him or her to join you in this exercise or keep a similar binder for him- or herself. Set a regular time to consult with each other about new ideas and information.

Planning Ahead

Once retired, you have your whole life ahead of you. For many, this can be just *too* big of an idea. Thinking about and organizing how to use your time to tackle issues that range from household chores to selling your home and moving—and everything in between—will be one useful way to consider the larger topic of retirement.

Use the next entry to think about those things you've wanted to do but haven't had the time (or perspective) to do until now. This entry will help you better understand both those things and yourself. After you've written your list, use the keys below to organize, code, and better understand the list.

THIRTY THINGS

1. Create a list of thirty things you want to do after retirement. Create your whole list *first*, writing one item on each line provided below until you've named thirty things you want to do.

2. Once you've written the entire list, return to each individual item and assign one of these categories to each item:

ED: Educational (returning to school, taking courses, workshops, etc.)

FA: Family (activity involving spouse, kids, grandkids, for instance)

FI: Financial (things connected with budgeting, investing, financial security)

FP: Fun/Play (things just for personal pleasure)

IS: Identity/Self-Esteem (things that improve self-image or create life direction)

MH: Mental Health (counseling, therapy, attending a support group)

MT: Maintenance Tasks (painting the house, spring cleaning, etc.)

MO: Moving (looking into selling your home and moving to a new location)

PH: Physical Health (things intended to improve or maintain your health)

PI: Personal Improvement (reading, learning a new skill, etc.)

RE: Relationships (things directly connected to building or maintaining relationships)

SR: Spiritual/Reflective (things most associated with a search for meaning)

TR: Travel (getting up and visiting all those places you've been itching to get to)

OT: Other (things that can't be placed under any other category)

3. Next, prioritize each item as:

A: crucial

B: important

C: less important

D: dispensable

4. Finally, assign a time line for when you'd like to do each thing:

1: within twenty-four hours

2: within a week

3: within a month

4: within a year

5: no time limit

Thing I Want to Do	Category	Priority	Time Line

Thing I Want to Do	Category	Priority	Time Line
_____	____	____	____
_____	____	____	____
_____	____	____	____
_____	____	____	____
_____	____	____	____

5. Take a look at your pattern of choices. How many of your choices were related to spending time with your family, how many were play items, how many represent major life changes, and so on? Tally up the way you classified each thing here.

__Educational	__Mental Health	__Relationships
__Family	__Maintenance Tasks	__Spiritual/Reflective
__Financial	__Moving	__Travel
__Fun/Play	__Physical Health	__Other
__Identity/Self-Esteem	__Personal Improvement	

6. Do you notice a pattern? Is there an even distribution of things in every category, or do most items fall into two or three areas? Describe the pattern.

_____

_____

_____

_____

7. Whatever the pattern, what does your list tell you about yourself?

_____

_____

_____

_____

8. Now look at your priority and your time line scores from your list of thirty things. What patterns do you see here, and what do they tell you?

_____

_____

_____

_____

_____

THINGS TO THINK ABOUT

- Were you able to come up with a list of thirty things you want to do? if not, why not?
- Were you surprised at the patterns or priorities that the list showed? Does anything concern or bother you about your list? What aspects of the list most please you?
- Are you ready to start doing some of the things on your list? If not, why not?

New Roads to Travel

Can you see an opportunity to take a different fork in the road or to create new forks? In fact, is it that the forks in the road are there and you're just not seeing them? Are there new interests waiting to be discovered—a major move, a new relationship, travel or adventure, a new job or volunteer work, an adult education course, or a new social activity of some kind? Whichever new road you take, and whenever you take it, perhaps it will lead nowhere or you won't like where it's taking you, and you'll turn back. Perhaps it will lead to a whole new set of roads you never imagined were there or available to you.

But, discovery usually requires some vision. Most explorers set out to discover something they suspected was there in the first place rather than just setting out, hoping to stumble onto a discovery. Having some vision of where you'd like your roads to

Discovery usually requires some vision. Most explorers set out to discover something they suspected was there in the first place rather than just setting out, hoping to stumble onto a discovery. Having some vision of where you'd like your roads to lead can provide some direction.

lead can provide some direction. As you think about your life and where you'd like to go, you'll need to think more specifically.

Recruiting Support

Your choices won't be carried out in a vacuum. As you've already identified in several journal entries, some of the changes you may be thinking about making will affect other people also, such as your spouse or children.

For instance, if your goal is to climb Mount Everest, start a business, or write a book, it will take lots of time, money, and effort. That's time, money, and effort that might have been directed toward your family and friends. Hopefully, these important people in your life will support you in your goals and won't resent your priorities. But the potential for resentment is there, especially if you don't explain what it is you're trying to do and why.

To deal with the practical politics of the situation, enlist the help and support of your family and friends whenever possible, including your spouse or partner, children, parents, friends, and other people whose support, assistance, and blessing will be important for success as you move along with your plans for change.

To deal with the practical *politics* of the situation, enlist the help and support of your family and friends whenever possible, including your spouse or partner, children, parents, friends, and other people whose support, assistance, and blessing will be important for success as you move along with your plans for change.

If you do need to win the support of other people, and you probably will, start early. Explain to them how you arrived at your goals, why the goals are important to you, and why you need their support and even participation.

Balancing Goals against Reality

Goal setting is important, but *realistic* goal setting is even more essential. Your goals should be meaningful but also workable. Part of successful retirement planning is choosing among alternatives and selecting the choice most likely to meet your goal.

If climbing Mount Everest is your goal, but neither your heart condition nor your budget will allow it, don't beat yourself up lamenting your fate. If moving to a South Seas island is your fondest desire, but you're the only one who can care for your aging father, come up with a Plan B. And there's *always* a Plan B. There's always a way to ally your goals with practicality. Perhaps instead of climbing Mount Everest, you could climb a lesser peak, or not climb at all but instead write a book about great climbers throughout history. Maybe instead of moving to the South Seas you could scrimp in some other areas to raise money to hire a caregiver for your father while you take an extended vacation to Bora Bora.

Ask yourself what factors most limit your individual goals. If it's money, can you do a better job of budgeting? Can you take a part-time job? Can you sell some assets? Should you enlist a financial consultant to help improve your income stream? Can you choose to do without some things to free up money to do what you'd most enjoy? If the most limiting factor is your health, what can you do about that? Ask your doctor what would be a safe substitute goal for someone in your condition. Is there a way to work up to the level of conditioning you'd need? Are there new prosthetic devices or medicines or surgeries that would help you accomplish your objective? In short, before you jettison any dreams, make sure you've explored all the options. Don't adopt an all-or-nothing mind-set.

Activating Your Plan

Having come this far and learned to know yourself better, your task now is to move on with the rest of your life. You can begin to translate your needs and goals into specific actions. Throughout this book, you've been identifying problems and opportunities. Now is the time to commit to a plan of personal growth for your-

Think of your plan as a living document, not one that's cut in stone, and get in the habit of periodically updating your plan.

self, as an individual, a partner, a family member, and a participant in your community.

If you're like most people, you'll change your plan often. Your interests and desires will evolve, and your circumstances will likely change as well. So think of your plan as a living document, not one that's cut in stone, and get in the habit of periodically updating your plan. Remember that retirement is always a work in progress, requiring continuous attention. So remain flexible and note that shorter-term plans (quarterly, monthly, weekly, and even daily) can, and probably *should,* be important as part of your master plan.

One way to think of this process is to liken yourself to an architect. The architect plans a building; you are planning the rest of your life. Like the architect, you start with just a thought. You think about what you want *your* building to represent, then you rough out that idea on paper, fine tune it, and fill in the details. Like the architect, you want to the end result to be as close to perfection as possible. And, like the architect, you know enough to always keep an eraser handy.

Looking Back as You Move Ahead

As you move further into your life, what seems undone? You've had the chance to think about and express your feelings and thoughts about this passage in your life, explore your feelings and relationships, and explore and understand your needs and goals. What's still undone or unsaid? As you near the end of this journal, it's important to provide a way to wrap up this part of your journey, even as you move on into your future. For all you've said and written already, what still needs to be said? What do you want to say about how you're feeling *now* that you've been through your healing journey, and how it's affected you?

REFLECTIONS ON YOUR JOURNEY

1. *I've learned . . .* _____

_____

_____

_____

_____

_____

2. *My journey through retirement has taught me . . .* _____

_____

_____

_____

_____

_____

3. *My journey through retirement has left me feeling . . .* _____

_____

_____

_____

_____

_____

4. *The most bitter part of my journey has been . . .* _____

_____

_____

_____

_____

5. The sweetest part of my journey has been . . . _____

_____

_____

_____

_____

_____

6. I most look forward to . . . _____

_____

_____

_____

_____

_____

7. I most need to say . . . _____

_____

_____

_____

_____

_____

THINGS TO THINK ABOUT

- What has this journey taught you about yourself and your life in general?
- Are you feeling prepared to move on with your retirement and your new life?

14

As One Journey Ends, Another Begins

OUR LATER YEARS can free us to take the biggest risks of our lives. With our children usually on their own, our career largely a thing of the past, and our fear of dying young no longer an inhibiting factor, we can take risks we might never have considered a few decades earlier.

You may choose to follow your dreams, whatever they are, because you're no longer burdened with fear of failure or a need to meet someone else's standards. Hopefully the work that you've completed in this journal has encouraged you and helped you to assess where you've been and where you want to go. Think of yourself as liberated.

Dealing with Difficulty

Retirement, like every other phase of life, holds the potential for tragedies big and small along with triumphs. Many of the unpleasant realities faced by retirees have to do with the loss of something or someone important to them: their health, the death of a loved one, or the disintegration of their family. Like

flowers, families don't stay the same forever. Our children, in whom we may have invested so much, grow up and often move away. Our parents age and pass on. Our siblings may grow distant under the pressure of their own lives. And the loss of a loved one is probably the most predictable, and most wrenching, setback. It's inevitable that we will experience loss and feel grief.

What isn't inevitable, however, is how prepared you are for these ups and downs and how you'll deal with them. Sometimes you may need professional help in confronting a crisis, especially if your usual ways of coping are not helping or are even causing the problem. For example, if your experience of loss drives you deeper and deeper into loneliness and despair, a minister, psychologist, social worker, or other human-relations professional might be able to help.

Retirement, like every other phase of life, holds the potential for tragedies big and small along with triumphs.

Important Work Remains to Be Done

The truth is, not all the important work of your life will be completed when you retire. Will you have the courage to try to complete that circle? The missing link might be some physical achievement such as exploring a far-off place, or something as mundane, but no less difficult, as making peace at last with an estranged friend.

In a society that values achievement, power, and possessions, some of the most important work a retiree can do is to develop a sense of who he or she really is and grasp the meaning of his or her life. No longer having the need to *climb* mountains, so to speak, you can take the time to enjoy the mountains' beauty instead, and reflect on their magnificence. If you are involved in valued activities and relationships, your retirement years will be marked by vitality, not emptiness. Peace of mind comes from being at one with yourself and with the people and circumstances of your world. It means accepting life as it is and always has been.

In the final analysis, peace of mind for the retiree comes not by withdrawing into either frenzied or lifeless inactivity, but by reaching out and actively pursuing a fitting capstone for his or her life's odyssey.

Tomorrow's Handles

Increased longevity is one of the striking developments of the twentieth century. Lifespans have grown more in the last century than in the previous five thousand years. So older adults are living longer and, generally speaking, living better. How do we handle this gift of added time?

"Every tomorrow has two handles," wrote Henry Ward Beecher. "We can take hold of it with the handle of anxiety or the handle of faith. We should live for the future, and yet should find our life in the . . . present."

Life is complex. There's no magic formula, no radical surgery, and no pill or simple insight that can stop the clock and give you back your youth. But you can shape the future. You can decide whether your will is to really *live* or just exist. "We are in great measure the architects of our added years," said Ethel Percy Andrus, founder of the AARP, and "it is within our power to enrich our later years by maintaining wholesome personal contact with our fellows and by using our leisure time in some useful activity."

Peace of mind for the retiree comes not by withdrawing into either frenzied or lifeless inactivity, but by reaching out and actively pursuing a fitting capstone for his or her life's odyssey.

Where to Now?

In completing this book, you've accomplished a great deal and taken important and significant steps down the path to a successful retirement. Where will your life take you now? If you've used your retirement journal as suggested, it has served many purposes: a place to express and explore feelings, a guide to thinking about the past and planning your future, and an aid to sorting out your thoughts and shaping your decisions.

Perhaps you've been able to use it as a mirror to reflect on your relationships and make them better and as a lens to see yourself and the world around you in a new way. If you've found the entries in this journal useful, you may want to explore *The Healing Journey* or *The Healing Journey for Couples*. Both of these books provide more general journal-writing exercises that are focused on self-exploration and personal growth. There are also other *Healing Journey* books in this series focused on specific issues such as grief, divorce, job loss, and menopause.

MY JOURNAL

1. How has your journal been most useful?

_____

_____

_____

_____

_____

_____

2. Have certain types of journal entries been more useful than others?

_____

_____

_____

_____

_____

3. What's been the most difficult aspect of journaling for you?

_____

_____

_____

_____

_____

4. What's been the most fulfilling aspect of journaling?

_____

_____

_____

_____

_____

5. Overall, describe your experience keeping this journal.

_____

_____

_____

_____

_____

6. *My journal* . . . _____

_____

_____

_____

_____

_____

_____

_____

- Have you enjoyed keeping a journal? If you've kept a journal before, what was different about this journal?
- Will you continue to use a journal in the future? If so, will you only keep a journal under special circumstances, or will you keep a daily journal?

Happiness as a Way of Traveling

"I want to be thoroughly used up when I die, for the harder I work, the more I live. Life is no brief candle for me. It is a sort of splendid torch which I have got hold of for the moment, and I want to make it burn as brightly as possible before handing it on to future generations."

——GEORGE BERNARD SHAW

Much of what you find on your journey will depend on how you look at it. Whether you see problems or challenges is largely up to you. Happiness is not so much a *destination* as it is a way of traveling.

An old business axiom says there are three kinds of people: those who make things happen, those who have things happen to them, and those who wonder, "What happened?" The purpose of this book has been to help you get yourself into that first category. How you proceed from here will determine your success.

Acknowledgments

Many thanks always to Kelly Franklin, our publisher at John Wiley & Sons. Kelly brought the Healing Journey series into reality and has served to guide and shape each book in the series. Thanks also to the great editing and production team at Wiley, who work hard to turn these manuscripts into books, and especially Sasha Kintzler, the Associate Managing Editor, and Dorothy Lin, our Associate Editor.

From Dorothy: My sincere appreciation to my good friends who graciously shared significant parts of their lives with me.

From Phil: I look forward to one day retiring with my wife and great friend of many years, Bev Sevier, for whom I am ever grateful. Only she could put up with me. And I'm constantly thankful for my wonderful daughter, Kaye, who really is my bundle of joy, and who will one day have a great career of her own.

About the Authors

DOROTHY MADWAY SAMPSON is a licensed clinical social worker with an MSS degree from Smith College, School for Social Work, and certification in Preretirement Education and Planning from the Andrus Gerontology Center at the University of Southern California. Thirty years ago, she and her husband took early retirement and moved with their four children to La Jolla, California. There, surrounded by many retirees who were financially secure, she became interested in the plethora of psychological challenges they were facing. She developed several courses in life-planning for retirement, which were presented at adult education classes and to major corporations throughout the country, including the Central Intelligence Agency. In addition to lecturing, she has served as chair of the Advisory Committee of the Retired Senior Volunteer Program of San Diego County. Presently she serves on the Community Board of Advisors of the Stein Institute for Research on Aging at the University of California, San Diego.

DALE FETHERLING has written, edited, or coauthored more than a dozen nonfiction books, ranging from biographies to self-help to history. Formerly a journalist with the *Los Angeles Times* and the *Minneapolis Tribune,* he has also taught writing and editing at four colleges and universities. He lives in San Diego.

PHIL RICH, EdD, MSW, DCSW, holds a doctorate in applied behavioral and organizational studies and is a clinical social work diplomate. Over the past two decades he has worked as a director of treatment programs, a clinical supervisor, and a practicing therapist in both the outpatient and inpatient setting. He currently maintains a private practice in western Massachusetts, in addition to his position as a clinical director. Phil is the primary author and series editor of the seven books in the Healing Journey series.